Cambridge Elements

Elements in Behavioural and Experimental Economics
edited by
Nicolas Jacquemet
University Paris-1 Panthéon Sorbonne and the Paris School of Economics
Olivier L'Haridon
Université de Rennes 1

PUBLIC FINANCE WITH BEHAVIOURAL AGENTS

Raphaël Lardeux
Insee and CRED Université Paris II

CAMBRIDGE
UNIVERSITY PRESS

Shaftesbury Road, Cambridge CB2 8EA, United Kingdom

One Liberty Plaza, 20th Floor, New York, NY 10006, USA

477 Williamstown Road, Port Melbourne, VIC 3207, Australia

314–321, 3rd Floor, Plot 3, Splendor Forum, Jasola District Centre,
New Delhi – 110025, India

103 Penang Road, #05–06/07, Visioncrest Commercial, Singapore 238467

Cambridge University Press is part of Cambridge University Press & Assessment,
a department of the University of Cambridge.

We share the University's mission to contribute to society through the pursuit of
education, learning and research at the highest international levels of excellence.

www.cambridge.org
Information on this title: www.cambridge.org/9781009014229

DOI: 10.1017/9781009029087

First published 2022

A catalogue record for this publication is available from the British Library.

ISBN 978-1-009-01422-9 Paperback
ISSN 2634-1824 (online)
ISSN 2634-1816 (print)

Public Finance with Behavioural Agents

Elements in Behavioural and Experimental Economics

DOI: 10.1017/9781009029087
First published online: December 2022

Raphaël Lardeux
Insee and CRED Université Paris II

Author for correspondence: Raphaël Lardeux, raphael.lardeux@outlook.fr

Abstract: Recent developments in behavioural economics have deeply influenced the way governments design public policies. They give citizens access to online simulators to cope with tax and benefits systems and increasingly rely on nudges to guide individual decisions. The recent surge of interest in behavioural public finance is grounded on the conviction that a better understanding of individual behaviours could improve predictions of tax revenue and help design better-suited incentives to save for retirement, search for a new job, go to school or seek medical attention. Through a presentation of the most recent developments in behavioural public finance, this Element discusses the way behavioural economics has improved our understanding of fiscal policies.

Keywords: public finance, behavioural bias, identification, sufficient statistics, structural model

ISBNs: 9781009014229 (PB), 9781009029087 (OC)
ISSNs: 2634-1824 (online), 2634-1816 (print)

Contents

1 Introduction

Recent developments in behavioural economics (BE) have deeply influenced the way governments design public policies. They give citizens access to online simulators to cope with tax and benefits systems and increasingly rely on *nudges* to guide individual decisions. Far beyond traditional instruments, the Covid-19 pandemic illustrates the large array of public health interventions available to support the vaccination campaign, from nudges to government mandates, including education, financial incentives and vaccination certificates with QR codes.[1] Finding the best policy requires an investigation of individual behaviours in order to understand the reasons for compliance.

The last decade has seen a surge in behavioural public finance (BPF). Beyond a taste for the foundation of public finance (PF) on cognitive sciences, this field of economic research is grounded on the conviction that a better understanding of individual behaviours could improve predictions of tax revenue and help design better-suited incentives to save for retirement, search for a new job, go to school or seek medical attention. Because behavioural agents may react in unpredictable ways, an examination of individual psychology quantitatively matters for the design of fiscal policies. Loss-averse US taxpayers facing a positive balance due on tax day are more eager to engage in tax-reducing activities, which results in a $1.4 billion loss of tax revenue (Rees-Jones, 2017). In contrast, procrastination on fiscal deductions costs US taxpayers around $50 million (Slemrod et al., 1997). A simple mailing sent by Bhargava and Manoli (2015) to inform 35,000 Californian tax filers about their eligibility to the Earned Income Tax Credit (EITC) led to refund claims totalling $4 million. The adoption of Electronic Toll Collection (ETC) raised tolls by 20 to 40 per cent because they are less salient for drivers (Finkelstein, 2009). The choice of a financially dominated health plan, which is more expensive regardless of how much care the employee requires, can cost each worker as much as $372 a year without additional health coverage (Bhargava et al., 2017).

Through a presentation of the most recent developments in BPF, this Element discusses the way BE has improved our understanding of fiscal policies. In contrast to traditional economic agents, behavioural agents have non-standard preferences or misperceive their economic environment. As a consequence, they may take different actions when faced with the same choice set. However, they can still be deemed rational since, conditional on modelling assumptions regarding their biases, their choices are consistent and predictable.

---

[1] On this topic, see the column 'More than nudges are needed to end the pandemic', published on 5 August 2021, by Nobel Prize–winner Richard Thaler in the *New York Times*.

Throughout this presentation, various psychological deviations will be encountered, including misperceptions, limited attention, beliefs, reference dependence, present bias, mental accounting, default option and representativeness, and we will analyse their consequences across different areas of PF, including taxation, unemployment insurance, health insurance, retirement and education. Rather than an extended survey of each topic, this Element is structured as a guide through the introduction of behavioural agents in PF, from estimable models to policy conclusions. Over the course of this presentation, some seminal issues are highlighted in order to illustrate how behaviour-oriented models could help improve fiscal policy design.[2]

Introducing the toolbox of an applied behavioural economist, this Element discusses the advantages and drawbacks of the two principal approaches in empirical PF: structural models and sufficient statistics. Interpretation of individual actions as *behavioural deviations* requires a deep understanding of informational environments. To this end, the analyst can rely on a wide range of empirical material, from lab experiments to natural experiments and survey to administrative data. Recent methodological developments in public policy evaluation offer powerful tools to recover convincing evidence of behavioural biases.

This Element builds on a wide literature at the intersection of PF and BE.[3] DellaVigna (2009) provides an overview of psychological biases and Congdon et al. (2011) discuss their consequences for policy design in the main areas of PF. To complement the empirical perspective adopted in this Element, Bernheim and Taubinsky (2018) present the core behavioural public economics models and summarise the underlying welfare principles developed in Bernheim (2009) and Bernheim and Rangel (2009). Farhi and Gabaix (2020) revisit the standard theories of optimal direct and indirect taxation with behavioural agents and further include nudges as available fiscal instruments. Other insightful references on public policies and psychological deviations include McCaffery and Slemrod (2006), Kirchler and Braithwaite (2007), Diamond and Vartiainen (2012), Mullainathan et al. (2012), Chetty (2015) and Gabuthy et al. (2021).

A deeper investigation of specific areas in PF can be found in Frank (2012) and Chandra et al. (2019) for behavioural health economics, Aaron (1999) and

---

[2] A large literature in BE investigates the design of properly behavioural fiscal policies through nudges, among which: Thaler and Sunstein (2003); Sunstein and Thaler (2009); Sunstein (2014); OECD (2017); Farhi and Gabaix (2020); Gabuthy et al. (2021). Although the final section briefly evokes nudges, this Element mostly focuses on traditional fiscal instruments.

[3] For a refresher on PF, see Salanié (2011); Auerbach and Feldstein (2013); Gruber (2015) and Atkinson and Stiglitz (2015).

Beshears et al. (2018) for behavioural retirement policies, Schnellenbach and Schubert (2015) for behavioural public choice and Lavecchia et al. (2016) for behavioural education. Since they have already been largely discussed by an extensive literature in BE, some topics are not covered by this Element. They are mostly related to prosocial behaviours, other-regarding preferences, self-image and signalling, in particular tax avoidance and tax evasion (Andreoni et al., 1998; Slemrod, 2007; Jacquemet et al., 2020), as well as public goods (Ledyard, 1995).

This Element deals with the following questions: Why should we care about psychological deviations in PF? How can we take them into account in theoretical models? Under which conditions can we identify and estimate their magnitude? How is it possible to disentangle behavioural deviations from incomplete information? When do we need to identify precisely the type of behavioural bias? What are the resulting guidelines for policymakers? Should individual biases be corrected?

After a presentation of the original model of optimal income taxation developed by James Mirrlees, Section 2 introduces the sufficient statistics approach to welfare analysis in PF. On top of a simpler derivation of PF models, this methodology enables the expression of optimal taxes and transfers as a function of estimable 'sufficient statistics', among which elasticities play a central role in capturing behavioural responses to fiscal incentives.

In traditional PF, these elasticities are estimated under strong assumptions regarding individual rationality and may therefore not be invariant to the way policies are framed. In order to explain the discrepancy between observed behavioural responses and their predicted theoretical counterpart, PF models started featuring behavioural agents who misperceive their environment or have non-standard preferences. Such behavioural deviations have first-order welfare effects and alter individual responses to fiscal reforms. These theoretical developments, presented in Section 3, ground a basis for the following empirical investigation.

Section 4 brings the theory of PF with behavioural agents to data. This section starts with a discussion of the conditions for the identification of these behavioural deviations. In order to be relevant for public finances, the analysis of informed choices from behavioural agents should take into account the conditions of the choice (*frames*) within public systems. As evidenced by Saez (2009), subjects do not respond in the same way to a subsidy depending on whether it is framed as a matching contribution or as a tax credit. Behavioural deviations can be revealed through changes in frames or mistakes, and should not possibly be rationalised by a standard economic model. In order to carry out this empirical step, this section presents a wide range of information sources, from lab experiments to survey and administrative data, the combination of which opens up the way to promising investigations. A last subsection deals with the estimation of structural models and sufficient statistics with behavioural agents. Structural estimations foster extrapolation while reduced-form causal estimates of sufficient statistics can be directly plugged in optimal formulas. Ultimately, the choice between these two methods depends on the necessity to specify the nature of the bias.

Section 5 concludes, with a discussion of fiscal policies targeting behavioural agents. Behavioural deviations fundamentally challenge the core notion of welfare and push the social planner to take a stand on bias correction. Determination of the optimal policy is even more delicate when biases are heterogeneous and potentially correlated with individual characteristics such as earnings. Fortunately, BPF broadens the scope of public action through choice architecture.

2 Behavioural Responses in Public Finance

In traditional PF, there are two main reasons why fiscal reforms consider individual behaviours: on the one hand, the prevention of undesirable behavioural responses to taxes and benefits, which would increase costs for public finances or generate a sub-optimal allocation of resources; on the other hand, to encourage or discourage specific behaviours.

The first category consists of distortions. One of the first lessons in PF is that by altering relative prices, taxes and benefits change individual choices. For instance, a targeted sales tax on some goods raises their price, which reduces demand for them and creates a deadweight loss. The second category is related to incentives. The government subsidises goods associated with positive externalities (culture, energy retrofit, infrastructures, etc.) and tries to keep citizens away from activities associated with negative externalities (consumption of alcohol or sugary drinks, pollution, etc.). Policies such as the EITC rely on the assumption that labour income subsidies can be efficient in stimulating job-seeking behaviours.

In both cases, the government has to understand and forecast individual behavioural responses to tax reforms. This section discusses the role of behavioural responses in standard PF, starting with a reminder on the traditional model of optimal income taxation.

2.1 The Mirrlees Model of Optimal Income Taxation

Market failures prevent market mechanisms from generating a Pareto optimal allocation, because individuals neglect the positive or negative repercussions of their actions (externalities), hold private information (information asymmetries) or would not engage in the production of a public good. In each of these situations, individual objectives are misaligned with social welfare, which provides a rationale for public intervention. For this purpose, the social planner relies on several instruments (taxes and transfers, quotas, production of public goods, market design, etc.) in order to influence or constrain individual actions towards a second-best equilibrium where the presence of market failures justifies the use of distortionary instruments.

The optimal income tax model developed by James Mirrlees (1971, 1986) lays the groundwork for the logic in public finance.[4] In this framework, the social planner levies taxes in order to redistribute income. Taxing away all earnings and giving the same lump-sum transfer to each agent would lead to a perfect redistribution level, but would also suppress incentives to work, which would drastically reduce tax revenue. Therefore, the social planner needs to set taxes in order to provide incentives for taxpayers to engage in productive activities.[5]

In the Mirrlees model, each individual is naturally endowed with a productivity level ω, which may be interpreted as the wage rate[6] they can get on the labour market. An hour of work will be more or less productive depending on this level. Given this *productivity type*, the agent chooses a work effort such that their *marginal rate of substitution* (MRS) between consumption and leisure equals their marginal gain from work. A government that has the ability to design type-specific income taxes would be able to influence work efforts through the control of this marginal gain. However, the social planner is not able to observe either individual levels of productivity or effort. If it were setting income taxes this way, the most productive agents would have an incentive to act as if they were less productive than they really are in order to pay a lower tax. This classic issue of adverse selection could strongly impact public finances.

Hence, the government faces an equity–efficiency trade-off: it tries to levy taxes in order to redistribute income between agents endowed with different productivity levels but cannot directly observe these productivity types. The core idea behind the Mirrlees model is that the social planner should design the optimal income tax schedule as a *truthful mechanism*, such that when faced with

---

[4] This presentation of the Mirrlees model is strongly based on chapter 4 of Salanié (2011). I urge readers interested in the proof of this model or theoretical developments in the economics of taxation to refer to this book.

[5] This framework, presented in terms of labour income taxation, naturally extends to all direct taxes and transfers depending on primary income, such as payroll taxes and means-tested benefits.

[6] Assuming that, in a competitive labour market, each worker is paid their productivity level. This productivity level captures several ideas, including social reproduction and unequal access to education (Saez and Stantcheva, 2016).

this tax schedule, each agent chooses the effort level that maximises social welfare for their productivity type.[7] Ultimately, efficiency is restored in a second-best economy with adverse selection.

Introducing notations helps develop a more precise representation of this model. Workers characterised by a productivity type ω who engage in a work effort l earn a gross income $z = \omega l$. A highly productive worker making a low effort can reach the same earnings level as a low-productivity worker who makes a high effort. Productivity types are distributed according to $F(\omega)$, with a density $f(\omega)$. Workers have standard preferences represented by utility[8] functions $u(c, z|\omega)$ conditional on their productivity types, increasing in consumption c and decreasing in work efforts (and thus in earnings z).[9] We further denote by $u_1(c, z|\omega)$ and $u_2(c, z|\omega)$ the partial derivatives of this utility function with respect to its first and second arguments.

The government cannot observe individual types ω nor individual effort levels l. It only observes pre-tax earnings z and sets taxes $T(z)$ as a function of this quantity. The derivative of this tax function $T'(z)$ is the *marginal tax rate*, which is the tax rate on an additional unit of pre-tax earnings. In a *progressive*[10] tax schedule, the marginal tax rate is a non-decreasing function of earnings.

Faced with this tax schedule, agents with productivity ω maximise their utility under the budget constraint $c \leq z - T(z)$, which gives the usual first-order condition:

$$1 - T'(z) = -\frac{u_2(c(\omega), z(\omega)|\omega)}{u_1(c(\omega), z(\omega)|\omega)} = mrs(c(\omega), z(\omega)|\omega).$$

Taxpayers choose an earnings level such that their MRS between consumption and effort is equal to the *retention rate* $1 - T'(z)$, which captures their marginal gain from effort. This condition is not sufficient, since high-productivity types would have an incentive to pretend that their productivity is lower in order to pay less tax. Hence, in line with the revelation principle, the

---

[7] This solution is grounded on the *revelation principle*, which reduces the set of mechanisms implementing the social welfare function to the subset of incentive-compatible direct mechanisms such that agents truthfully report their productivity types. Hence, the social planner can reduce their search to incentive-compatible tax schedules.

[8] Since the standard economic theory makes no distinction between the experienced utility and the decision utility, the utility function u refers to a general utility concept in this section. These utility concepts are introduced in Section 3.

[9] Given the individual productivity type, it is virtually the same to consider that agents choose their work effort or their earnings level. In line with Saez (2001), we assume that workers maximise utility over earnings z.

[10] A progressive tax schedule is characterised by a marginal tax rate greater than or equal to the average tax rate for each pre-tax earnings level z, which includes convex tax schedules as well as linear tax schedules with a lump-sum transfer.

social planner chooses a pair of functions $(c(\omega), z(\omega))$ consistent with the following *incentive-compatibility constraint*:

$$\forall \omega, \omega' \; u(c(\omega), z(\omega)|\omega) \geq u(c(\omega'), z(\omega')|\omega),$$

which states that any agent with productivity ω should be better off with the allocation $(c(\omega), z(\omega))$ designed for their type than with any other allocation $c(\omega'), z(\omega')$ designed for any other type ω'. Now assume that the MRS between consumption and pre-tax income $mrs(c(\omega), z(\omega)|\omega)$ is decreasing with productivity ω. Intuitively, starting from a given pre-tax income, this condition stipulates that any increase in effort will be more painful and less rewarding for a low-productivity type than for a high-productivity type. Under this Spence-Mirrlees condition – also called the *single-crossing condition* since it implies that the indifference curves of two agents with different productivity levels cross only once in the (c, z) plan – more productive agents earn higher pre-tax earnings and consume more than lower-productivity types.

As depicted in Figure 1, an optimal tax schedule generates a separating equilibrium between different productivity types. The income tax schedule shows the feasible set of allocations (c, z). For a given productivity type, indifference curves display the set of consumption-earnings combinations providing the same utility level. An indifference curve further away in the upper

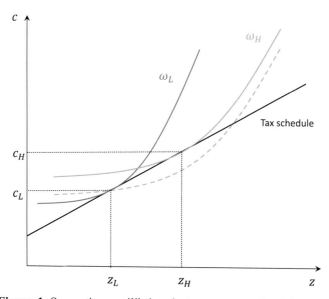

Figure 1 Separating equilibrium between two productivity types
Note: At the optimum, when faced with this tax schedule, the high-productivity type ω_H locates at a higher taxable income level z_H than the low-productivity type ω_L.

left quadrant is characterised by a higher utility level, since agents can consume a higher fraction of their earnings. A worker with productivity ω_L chooses an effort level associated with gross earnings z_L and gets a consumption level c_L. At (c_L, z_L), in line with the single-crossing condition, the MRS of a high-productivity worker characterised by $\omega_H > \omega_L$ is lower than the MRS of the low-productivity type. Hence, this worker will be better off taking the allocation (c_H, z_H) since they will be able to locate on an indifference curve characterised by a higher utility level. Under the Spence-Mirrlees condition, the tax schedule induces workers with different productivity types to choose different effort levels and consequently end up with different allocations. This separating equilibrium reveals their position in the distribution of productivity types.

Social welfare $W = \int_\omega G(u(c(\omega), z(\omega)|\omega))f(\omega)d\omega$ aggregates individual utilities using an increasing and concave function G that weights these utilities according to a redistributive objective. For instance, if G is the identity, the government has utilitarian preferences and maximises the unweighted sum of individual utilities. In contrast, Rawlsian preferences only consider the lowest utility level. The government is subject to a budget constraint, which states that government expenditures E cannot exceed tax revenue: $E \leq \int_z T(z)h(z)dz$, where $h(z)$ stands for the density of earnings at the optimum.

Finally, optimal income taxes maximise social welfare under the first-order conditions and the incentive-compatibility constraints for each productivity type ω as well as the budget constraint of the government. Derivation of this optimal schedule is complex, provides few insights and hardly seems related to empirical quantities. The next section presents the more recent *sufficient statistics* approach to optimal fiscal policies, which offers a nice way to overcome these issues.

2.2 The Sufficient Statistics Approach to Optimal Fiscal Policies

The *sufficient statistics* approach initiated by Piketty (1997), Saez (2001) and Chetty (2009) provides a reformulation of optimal policy instruments as a function of empirically estimable sufficient statistics. Chetty (2009) characterises this methodology as a 'bridge between structural and reduced-form methods'. Instead of designing fiscal instruments from scratch, this approach considers a small reform which is compensated by lump-sum transfers, such that the government budget remains constant. In this way, any change in instruments is directly related to welfare variations. The consequences of this small reform on tax revenue can be summarised by a *mechanical effect* and a *behavioural effect*, which represent the main forces at play in the determination of optimal instruments. The *mechanical effect* captures variations in tax revenue assuming individual decisions remain unchanged. However, a tax reform generally alters individual incentives, inducing agents to modify their choices. The *behavioural effect* catches the impact of such adjustments on tax revenue. This distinction proves very useful when bringing tax theory to data.

Beyond direct taxation, this sufficient statistics approach has been extended to a wider range of taxes and public transfers. It proves particularly useful to evaluate marginal welfare gains from policy changes. We review here the most famous applications of sufficient statistics formulas for labour income taxation, indirect taxation and unemployment insurance. Chetty (2009) and Kleven (2021) provide an extended presentation of this methodology. Sections 3, 4 and 5 build on these formulas to introduce behavioural agents.

2.2.1 Optimal Direct Income Taxation

Saez (2001) develops a very clear and practical solution of the Mirrlees model based on the sufficient statistics approach. As shown in Section 2.1, social welfare can be given by:

$$W = \int_z \left\{ G\Big(u(z - T(z), z|\omega)\Big) + \lambda[T(z) - E]\right\}h(z)dz, \tag{1}$$

where the multiplier λ associated with the budget constraint of the government is the *marginal value of public funds*. Saez (2001) defines the social marginal welfare weight at earnings z as $g(z) = G'(u)u_c/\lambda$. This weight represents the utility value for the government to transfer one additional euro to an agent with earnings z. In order to simplify the derivations, we further assume no income effect.

Starting from the optimal tax schedule, consider a small increase $d\tau$ in the marginal tax rate over a small income range between z^* and $z^* + dz^*$. Such a small variation in the tax rate around the optimum should have no first-order effect on welfare but has two consequences on tax revenue:

- A *mechanical effect*: each taxpayer above z^* pays additional taxes $d\tau dz^*$. Hence, this reform mechanically increases total tax revenue by $d\tau dz^* \lambda \int_{z>z^*} h(z)dz$ but induces welfare losses $-d\tau dz^* \lambda g(z)$ for agents above earnings z^*, resulting in a total mechanical effect given by: $d\tau dz^* \lambda \int_{z>z^*}(1 - g(z))h(z)dz$.
- A *behavioural effect*: a mass $\int_{z^*}^{z^*+dz^*} h(z)dz \approx dz^* h(z^*)$ of taxpayers faced with a higher marginal tax rate in an income range between z^* and $z^* + dz^*$ have

an incentive to adjust their earnings downwards. Above this range, absent any income effect, agents do not adjust their taxable income. Around the optimal tax schedule, there are no first-order consequences of this adjustment through individual preferences, but the impact through the government budget constraint is given by: $-\lambda \int_{z^*}^{z^*+dz^*} T'(z)\frac{\partial z}{\partial(1-\tau)}\, d\tau\, h(z)\, dz$. Saez (2001) defines the elasticity of taxable income with respect to the retention rate as $\varepsilon(z) = \frac{\partial z}{\partial(1-\tau)}\frac{1-\tau}{z}$, with $\tau = T'(z)$ the marginal tax rate at z. Using approximations for dz^* small enough,[11] the behavioural effect is given by: $-\lambda\varepsilon(z^*)\frac{T'(z^*)}{1-T'(z^*)}z^* d\tau dz^* h(z^*)$.

The marginal welfare effect dW of a small variation in the income tax rate $d\tau$ is equal to the sum of the mechanical and the behavioural effects:

$$dW = \underbrace{d\tau dz^* \lambda \int_{z>z^*}\left(1-g(z)\right)h(z)dz}_{mechanical\ effect} - \underbrace{\lambda\varepsilon(z^*)\frac{T'(z^*)}{1-T'(z^*)}z^* d\tau dz^* h(z^*)}_{behavioural\ effect}.$$

Factoring common terms, this equation simplifies to:

$$\frac{1}{\lambda dz^*}\frac{dW}{d\tau} = \int_{z>z^*}\left(1-g(z)\right)h(z)dz - \frac{T'(z^*)}{1-T'(z^*)}\varepsilon(z^*)z^* h(z^*).$$

Equating this marginal welfare effect to zero provides the optimal tax formula presented by Saez (2001):

$$\frac{T'(z^*)}{1-T'(z^*)} = \frac{1}{\varepsilon(z^*)z^* h(z^*)}\int_{z>z^*}\left(1-g(z)\right)h(z)dz.$$

Since the right-hand side of this equation is always non-negative, marginal tax rates are always between 0 and 1. They are higher when the social value $g(z|z > z^*)$ of an additional euro transferred to taxpayers with earnings above z^* is low, when few people are concerned by this distortion ($h(z^*)$ small) and when these people are not too responsive to variations in marginal tax rates ($\varepsilon(z^*)$ small). In conclusion, empirical estimates for the elasticity of taxable income $\varepsilon(z^*)$ are crucial to evaluate the optimality of an income tax schedule.

---

[11] When agents adjust their earnings by dz, the non-linear tax schedule changes by $T'' = T'dz$. As explained by Saez (2001), one consequence is that the density of earnings in the optimal tax formula is a virtual density that would exist if agents were optimising with respect to the linear tax schedule tangent to the non-linear tax schedule in z^*. For a didactic purpose, these technicalities are not developed here.

2.2.2 Optimal indirect taxation

According to Chetty (2009), the starting point of the sufficient statistics approach is the measurement of deadweight losses from commodity taxes, originating in the works of Harberger (1964). Consider a representative agent with quasi-linear utility $u(x) + y$, where x is the taxed good and y is the numeraire. The government collects taxes τx and gives them back through lump-sum transfers T. The budget constraint of the agent is: $y + (p + \tau)x \leq R + T$, where τ is the tax rate, p is the pre-tax producer price and R is the budget. Social welfare is given by:

$$W = u(x) + R - x(p + \tau) + T + \lambda[\tau x - T] \tag{2}$$

where the multiplier λ is the unit value of public funds. The optimal choice of lump-sum transfers by the government implies $\lambda = 1$. Taxes have no mechanical effects since taxation is neutral from a strict budgetary perspective. However, there is a behavioural effect stemming from the consumption response of the agent. The welfare consequences of this tax are therefore:

$$\frac{dW}{d\tau} = \tau \frac{dx}{d\tau} = x\varepsilon.$$

This famous Harberger formula for a first-order welfare loss can be expressed as a function of the elasticity $\varepsilon = \frac{dx/x}{d\tau/\tau}$ of quantities to the tax rate.[12] In particular, the sufficient statistics approach does not require the estimation of structural demand and supply elasticities.

2.2.3 Social Insurance

Beyond tax analysis, the sufficient statistics approach proves very useful for social insurance policy. We follow Baily (1978) and Chetty (2006, 2009) to illustrate this point in the case of optimal unemployment insurance. The logic can easily be extended to other situations of insurance involving moral hazard, wherein the agent can exert an unobservable effort in order to avoid a bad state, such as adopting a preventive and healthy behaviour in order to reduce the risks of lifestyle diseases or accidents.

Taxation involves redistribution of resources between different types of agents, while insurance is concerned with the redistribution of resources between different states. Consider a representative agent with utility of consumption $u(c)$ who exerts an effort e in order to avoid unemployment. As

---

[12] This simplified model leaves aside adjustments from the productive sector. Considering convex production costs and perfect competition, Chetty (2009) shows that the welfare consequences of a sales tax are given by the same equation, where elasticity ε captures adjustments of equilibrium quantities with respect to this tax from both the demand and the supply side of the market.

a result, they can either be employed with probability $p(e) = e$ or unemployed with probability $1 - e$.[13] The cost of effort is given by a twice-differentiable convex cost function $\psi(e)$. Consumption c_e is equal to labour income w net of taxes τ when employed, such that $c_e = w - \tau$, and equal to unemployment insurance (UI) benefits B when unemployed. To simplify notations, we can write $u'_e = u'(c_e)$ and $u'_u = u'(B)$. The expected utility of this agent is equal to $eu(w - \tau) + (1 - e)u(B) - \psi(e)$. The optimal effort level is such that the marginal cost of effort is equal to its marginal benefit: $\psi'(e) = u(w - \tau) - u(B)$.

The government budget constraint reflects the equality between taxes and benefits in expectations: $e\tau = (1 - e)B$ or, as a function of the duration unemployed, $\tau = BD$ with $D = \sum_{k=1}^{\infty}(1 - e)^t = (1 - e)/e$. The social welfare function is given by:

$$W = \{eu(w - \tau) + (1 - e)u(B) - \psi(e)\} + \lambda e[\tau - BD],$$

where, as for the case of income taxes, λ represents the marginal value of public funds. The first-order condition with respect to τ states that $\frac{\partial W}{\partial \tau} = -eu'(c_e) + \lambda e = 0$, which implies that $\lambda = u'_e$ in equilibrium. The marginal value of an additional euro of taxes is equal to the marginal utility cost of this euro being taxed away from the worker. Here again, the welfare impact dW of a small variation in benefits dB is the sum of two effects:

- A *mechanical effect*: in order to fully compensate the unit rise dB in unemployment benefits, the government raises taxes by DdB. The expected gain $(1 - e)u'_u dB$ if unemployed is balanced by an expected loss $-eu'_e DdB$ if employed. The total mechanical effect is therefore equal to $e(u'_u - u'_e)DdB$.
- A *behavioural effect*: higher unemployment benefits reduce incentives for unemployed workers to search for a new job, which increases unemployment duration and therefore the cost of UI by $D\varepsilon_D dB$, where $\varepsilon_D = \frac{\partial D}{\partial B}\frac{B}{D}$ is the elasticity of unemployment duration with respect to benefits. The government further increases taxes to compensate for this behavioural reaction, which has a first-order effect on utility while employed, as agents do not internalise the link between taxes and benefits in the budget of the government. The total behavioural effect is the expected loss: $-eu'_e\varepsilon_D DdB$.

The welfare impact of a small variation in unemployment benefits is given by:

---

[13] Following Chetty (2009), we assume for simplicity that units of e are chosen so that $p(e) = e$. In practice, job search activities depend on other external factors, such as labour market conditions, which implies that the unemployed workers cannot perfectly control their probability to find a new job. If it were the case, then a government observing unemployment duration would be able to directly control search effort, hence suppressing the moral hazard issue.

$$\frac{1 + D \, dW}{D \quad dB} = u'_u - u'_e - \varepsilon_D u'_e.$$

The optimal level of unemployment benefits should be set such that the welfare gain of insurance for unemployed workers $(u'_u - u'_e)/u'_e$ balances the efficiency loss from the moral hazard issue ε_D.[14] Using, as in Chetty (2006), a first-order approximation of the marginal utility and the definition of the coefficient of relative risk aversion $\gamma = -c_e u''_e/u'_e$, the replacement rate for unemployment benefits can be expressed as follows

$$\frac{B}{c_e} \approx 1 - \frac{\varepsilon_D}{\gamma}.$$

Unemployment benefits stand for a higher share of consumption from employment when moral hazard is low (low elasticity of unemployment duration ε_D) or when the insurance value is high (γ high, which means that agents are strongly risk averse). As explained by Chetty (2009), welfare evaluations of optimal UI do not rely on any assumptions regarding private insurance. An empirical evaluation of the optimal replacement rate for unemployment benefits just requires the estimation of two sufficient statistics: the coefficient of relative risk aversion γ and the elasticity ε_D of unemployment duration with respect to UI benefits.

2.3 Connecting Theory to Data

The recent popularity of the sufficient statistics approach in public finance stems from the seamless connection it makes between theory and empirics. These formulas directly express optimal instruments as a function of estimable statistics. Beyond the ease of derivation of the theoretical model, several advantages of this approach, already highlighted by Chetty (2009), should be stressed.

First, empirical moments can be directly plugged into the optimal formula without the need to estimate a complex structural model. They are 'sufficient' in that we do not have to know the 'primitives' of the model (individual preferences, production costs, productivity types, etc.) in order to derive welfare analysis. Second, the possibility to estimate these statistics separately from the theoretical model enables the use of reduced-form causal estimation methods, which is essential when it comes to predicting the costs of future fiscal reforms. Third, estimation of a full structural model generally involves recovering many parameters, which is not always necessary to derive a welfare analysis.

---

[14] This analysis disregards partial equilibrium effects. The marginal cost associated with a small increase in unemployment benefits could be lower in the case of a positive impact on the value of employment via wage adjustments. See Landais et al. (2018a, b) and Kroft et al. (2020) for a thorough welfare analysis of unemployment benefits with partial equilibrium effects.

From there on, the core issue becomes the estimation of welfare-relevant sufficient statistics. A very large empirical literature in PF has investigated individual responses to fiscal reforms. Interested readers may refer to Saez et al. (2012) for estimations of the elasticity of taxable income, Chetty and Finkelstein (2013) for social insurance and Schmieder and Von Wachter (2016) for UI.

Of course, the ease of use of the sufficient statistics approach comes at a cost. First, elasticities are endogenous to the fiscal instruments. Giving a value for the optimal level of taxes or unemployment benefits would require estimates of those sufficient statistics at the optimum, which is rarely feasible.[15] As an alternative, estimated sufficient statistics may indicate the direction of welfare variations dW. Then, it is possible to conclude whether an instrument should be adjusted upwards or downwards depending on its welfare impact. Landais et al. (2018a, b) provide an example of this methodology, deriving welfare analysis of optimal UI in a macroeconomic environment.

Second, as explained by Saez et al. (2012, p. 4), a relevant elasticity should be 'an accurate indicator of the revenue leakage due to behavioural responses', which captures all behavioural responses, including job search, itemised deductions and tax avoidance. If some adjustment margins are missing, the resulting parameter will not be relevant to forecast fiscal costs. Saez et al. (2012, p. 16) conclude that 'the taxable income elasticity depends not only on individual preferences, but also on the tax structure'. Consequently, an elasticity estimated in a tax environment with specific adjustment opportunities cannot immediately be transposed to another environment. On top of the shape of the tax schedule, the magnitude of the elasticity depends on whether taxpayers can adjust their labour supply, how many tax credits they can claim and how easily they can shift their income between different tax bases (for instance, choose to report their earnings as capital income or wages).

The sufficient statistics approach proves very useful in PF since it transparently connects behavioural responses to their welfare consequences. However, these individual reactions appear as a black box barely transposable to other situations. A growing literature in BPF shows that a deeper investigation of individual behaviours may improve the design of fiscal policies. The next sections review in detail the impact of psychological biases on individual behavioural responses and discuss their consequences for policy design.

---

[15] As a notable exception, Saez (2001) provides an explicit expression for the optimal top linear income tax rate because it depends on parameters which are constant when earnings are high enough (convergence result).

3 Public Transfers with Behavioural Agents

As do standard economic agents, behavioural agents make choices that maximise their utility under a budget constraint, which depends on prices and on their financial resources.[16] However, they *deviate* from the decision-making process of a standard economic agent: they have a distorted perception of their economic environment or do not consider their welfare-relevant preferences, for instance if they take too much into account the context of their decision in order to forecast their future welfare.

Behavioural deviations can have tremendous consequences for public policy design. Consider an elasticity estimated in a complex and opaque tax structure. Behavioural agents may display a low responsiveness to tax incentives either because they do not perceive these incentives or because they rationally choose not to assign too much time and cognitive capacity to these dimensions. Therefore, the estimated elasticity would probably be quite low. Now consider a salient and large tax reform that sheds light on some opaque attribute of this tax schedule. Following the logic of the previous section, the government uses the estimated elasticity and predicts moderate earnings responses. However, behavioural taxpayers, who used to ignore tax incentives, may start to pay attention to these features and display strong earnings responses, which would imply potentially large losses of tax revenue compared to the initial prediction of the government. Saez et al. (2012) suggest that elasticities estimated from large changes may be larger than elasticities estimated from small changes.

This section shows that investigating PF with behavioural agents helps to explain some puzzling empirical behaviours in order to ultimately improve the design of optimal policies. After a rapid overview of the psychological deviations characterising the differences between behavioural and traditional economic agents, we show how to include behavioural biases in PF models.

3.1 Standard Versus Behavioural Agents

A rational economic agent takes optimal actions that maximise their preferences under a budget constraint depending on information available in their environment.[17] This rationality assumption grounds the *Weak Axiom of Revealed Preferences* (WARP). This axiom states that when two bundles of goods, A and B,

---

[16] Recent empirical investigations question the ability of agents to engage in such a rational maximisation process (e.g. Bhargava et al., 2017). This Element focuses on agents who react to fiscal policies, which means that they formulate economic choices and that they take these policies into account (with potential misperceptions or misunderstandings).

[17] In a dynamic and uncertain environment, the agent considers their expected utility, forms beliefs about the outside world and actualises these beliefs in a Bayesian way.

are affordable, if bundle A is chosen over bundle B then the consumer reveals that they prefer bundle A and there are no circumstances under which bundle B would be strictly preferred over bundle A. As developed in section 2.F of Mas-Colell et al. (1995), a demand function $x(p, w)$ expressed as a function of a price-wealth pair (p, w) satisfies the WARP if, for any (p, w) and (p', w'):

$$\text{if } p.x(p', w') \leq w \quad \text{and} \quad x(p', w') \neq x(p, w), \quad \text{then} \quad p'.x(p, w) > w'.$$

In simpler terms, under price p and wealth w, the consumer chooses $x(p, w)$ over another bundle $x(p', w')$ even though this bundle is affordable, since $p.x(p', w') \leq w$. The WARP interprets this choice as revealing a preference for $x(p, w)$ over $x(p', w')$. Then, under the pair (p', w'), if the consumer chooses $x(p', w')$, it must be that $x(p, w)$ is not feasible, which implies that $p'.x(p, w) > w'$.

Revealed preferences theory ensures consistency between the set of choices an agent faces and the actions they take. This axiom has proved empirically useful to infer the local shape of preferences from changes in consumption following a variation in relative prices, without the need to recover the utility function as a whole. This 'principle of revealed preferences' is essential in PF to predict behavioural responses to changes in fiscal instruments.

However, BE has highlighted multiple examples of breaches of the WARP, such as choice inconsistencies, choice reversals, preference for dominated choices and preference for restricted choice sets (to avoid tempting goods or overflow of information). Without this axiom, identification of individual preferences and welfare analysis becomes impossible. Fortunately, BE has shown that, in many cases, choice consistencies can be recovered under explicit assumptions about the shape of behavioural biases.

3.1.1 Psychological Deviations

Rabin (2002) and DellaVigna (2009) provide a clear framework to characterise behavioural agents according to their psychological deviations from the decision process of a standard agent. In general, a utility maximising agent considers the following programme:

$$\max_{x_i^t \in X_i} \sum_{t=0}^{\infty} \delta^t \sum_{s_t \in S_t} p(s_t) u(x_i^t | s_t).$$

At time 0, they maximise their discounted expected utility with a discount factor δ and a probability distribution $p(s_t)$ over the set S_t of all possible states of the world s_t at time t. Conditional on a state of the world at time t, utility $u(x_i^t \mid s_t)$

is evaluated for each possible vector of actions x_i^t in the set of all possible strategies X_i.

Behavioural deviations from this program fall into two main categories, both of which are relevant in understanding individual responses to public policies. First, behavioural agents may have non-standard preferences. Self-control problems from myopic agents question the assumption of a time-consistent discount factor δ. Gains and losses are asymmetrically weighted by reference-dependent agents who evaluate their utility $u(x\,|\,s,r)$ conditional on a reference point r. Agents suffering from a projection bias place too much weight on the current state of the world s_t when making long-term decisions. Behavioural agents may also have some meta-preferences: preferences over the conditions of their decision or their choice set. For instance, people on a diet might prefer not being given the choice to eat unhealthy food at lunch.

Second, behavioural agents may form a wrong representation of their environment, either because they do not pay attention to or because they misperceive some relevant features of X_i, because they are influenced by the way alternatives are framed or because they use simplifying heuristics to cope with complex information. Optimistic and pessimistic agents mis-estimate probabilities $p(s_t)$.

3.1.2 Decision or Experienced Utility?

The WARP assumes that preferences guide and can therefore be recovered from choices. This traditional representation of a *decision utility* has been widely adopted in economics since individual choices can conveniently be modelled as decisions maximising preferences under a budget constraint. In this perspective, the decision utility appears as the relevant measure of preferences to predict future responses to changes in prices and fiscal instruments, and consequently to estimate an aggregate demand.

However, this decision utility may not be the right criterion to assess individual welfare. From a hedonic perspective, individual well-being would rather be associated with the utility that agents derive from the economic experience as a whole (Kahneman et al., 1999; Frey and Stutzer, 2002). A large literature in BE has shown this *experienced utility* to be 'empirically distinct from decision utility' (Kahneman et al., 1997, p. 376). Kahneman and Sugden (2005) advise basing economic evaluations on the experienced utility rather than on the decision utility. The experienced utility would be closer to a social welfare objective, provided that it can be observed and that the planner is willing to correct for behavioural biases resulting from the decision utility. The final section discusses these normative considerations.

3.1.3 Perception of the Economic Environment

The actions of a behavioural agent may depart from those of a standard agent if they form a distorted representation of their economic environment. Using large-scale surveys on a representative sample of the US population, Stantcheva (2021) illustrates a distorted view of the income and estate tax systems: respondents tend to underestimate tax progressivity and the share of households who do not pay income taxes, and believe that the estate tax exemption threshold is much lower than it is. In BPF, misperception of the environment can be divided into two broad categories: *salience* and *complexity*. Agents can miss some relevant features or underestimate them if they are not salient. When faced with a complex environment, they may simplify it or even take into account some irrelevant information.

Salience

Salience refers to the use of an available, known and relevant information during the decision process. The agent can be aware of a piece of information, report it perfectly during a survey but if this information is not sufficiently salient, they will forget to take it into account or underestimate its magnitude when making a choice.

Chetty et al. (2009) highlight a tremendous salience effect in the case of sales taxes. In US stores, price tags do not include the sales tax, which is only added to the bill at the register. According to economic theory, consumers should only take into account tax-inclusive prices, regardless of their components. In order to test this theory, Chetty et al. (2009) added tax-inclusive prices to posted prices. Whereas tax theory predicts no response, this intervention induced an 8 per cent drop in demand. Even though, as confirmed by a survey, consumers know the value of the sales tax rate, they appear to underestimate or forget about the sales tax when shopping. Making the tax-inclusive price salient corrects for their misperception bias, bringing their perceived budget constraint closer to the budget constraint of a fully attentive consumer. In a comparison of excise and sales taxes on cigarettes, Goldin and Homonoff (2013) found that all consumers respond to excise taxes, which are included in price tags, but only low-income consumers respond to sales taxes. Their result suggests that attention depends on how financially constrained consumers are. Low-income consumers face a high utility cost of optimisation errors, so they try harder to take register taxes into account in order to minimise this cost. Conversely, agents may develop selective attention in order to not pay attention to some salient but unpleasant feature, such as an empty bank account in Olafsson and Pagel (2017).

Complexity

The distinction between salience and complexity matters for policy recommendation, since a simple reminder such as tax-inclusive price tags can be highly efficient in shedding light on some opaque attribute in a simple environment, but much less so in a complex environment where agents can be confused by the accumulation of rules.

Public finance involve complex systems, characterised by many non-linear or recursive rules interacting with each other. A complex tax system characterised by multiple deductions (Kopczuk, 2005) has an ambiguous impact on individual decisions. On the one hand, complexity provides many avoidance opportunities (Slemrod and Kopczuk, 2002); on the other hand, agents may hardly perceived incentives (Abeler and Jäger, 2015). The starting point of the French income tax appears to be a relevant example of complexity. Tax filers only have to pay taxes if the amount due exceeds a tax collection minimum m. Therefore, in order to determine the threshold where tax liabilities start z_0, they have to solve the equation $t(z_0) = m$, where t is a piecewise linear tax schedule. Lardeux (2021) shows evidence of confusion among tax filers who (partially) neglect this tax collection minimum and end up bunching at an irrelevant threshold. In such complex environments, agents may develop heuristics in order to form a simpler mental representation of their decision environment. Asking 4,200 subjects to predict income taxes for different levels of taxable income, Rees-Jones and Taubinsky (2020) observe a tendency of US taxpayers to smooth the non-linear tax schedule, starting from their own taxable income and using their average tax rate instead of computing the effective tax schedule.

Welfare benefits depend on different notions of earnings, interact with each other in some ambiguous way and require frequent re-applications. Following the 2003 expansion of the Child and Dependent Care Credit (CDCC) that reduced the after-tax price of childcare, Miller and Mumford (2015) found that taxpayers increased their expenditures on childcare. This seemingly rational response completely ignored the less salient interactions with the Child Tax Credit (CTC), which often reduced or eliminated the childcare subsidy.

Complexity extends beyond tax and transfers in PF. Dynarski and Scott–Clayton (2006) explain that the complexity of student aid systems is a major obstacle for their optimal distribution. Personal assistance in completing the Free Application of Federal Student Aid (FAFSA) and information about the size of student aids provided by Bettinger et al. (2012) significantly and persistently raised college attendance.

3.2 Behavioural Models to Rationalise Individual Responses to Fiscal Policies

This subsection discusses the introduction of psychological deviations in the PF models presented in Section 2. Considering behavioural agents induces two major changes. First, small fiscal reforms have first-order welfare effects. Second, earnings responses from behavioural agents differ from those of standard agents.

3.2.1 Notations

In PF, the social planner maximises an aggregation of individual preferences. Normative considerations focus on the way individual preferences are aggregated (Saez and Stantcheva, 2016) but not on the nature of individual preferences. In the previous section, the general utility function u was introduced without discussion of how choices relate to welfare. In BPF, the social planner tries to achieve maximal well-being as measured by the *experienced utility* u and takes into account individual behavioural responses to fiscal reforms determined by their *decision utility* v. Utility functions u and v are twice-differentiable, concave and $u(x) \neq v(x)$ in general. This formulation may encompass a large range of non-standard preferences (reference-dependent preferences, present bias, projection bias, etc.).

In order to model biases related to a misperception of the economic environment (attention, optimism, mental accounting, etc.), Gabaix (2014) assumes that a behavioural agent makes the same choices as a standard agent maximising their decision utility subject to the economic environment perceived by the behavioural agent. The choice x_b of a behavioural agent with decision utility v who perceives prices p as p_b can be defined as:

$$x_b \equiv argmax\ v(x|p_b, R). \tag{3}$$

Thereafter, variables characterising behavioural agents are denoted by a subscript b.

3.2.2 Behavioural Taxation

Income Tax

Consider a behavioural agent of type ω characterised by the decision utility $v(c, z|\omega)$ without income effects, who misperceives the tax schedule $T(z)$ as $T_b(z)$. According to Equation (3), this agent chooses earnings z_b, such that

$\left(1 - T'_b(z_b)\right)v_1 + v_2 = 0$, where $v_1 \geq 0$ and $v_2 \leq 0$ refer to the partial derivatives of v with respect to its first and second arguments.[18]

As in Section 2, the government sets tax instruments in order to maximise welfare given by Equation (1), except that earnings z_b now encompass behavioural biases. The marginal welfare variation from a small reform around z_b^* is:

$$\frac{1}{\lambda dz^*}\frac{dW}{d\tau} = \int_{z_b > z_b^*} \left[1 - g(z_b) + \underbrace{\left(\frac{v_2}{v_1} - \frac{u_2}{u_1} + T'(z_b) - T'_b(z_b)\right)\frac{g(z_b)\varepsilon_b(z_b)z_b}{1 - T'(z_b)}}_{\text{behavioural wedge}} \right] h(z_b)dz_b$$

$$-\frac{T'(z_b^*)}{1 - T'(z_b^*)}\varepsilon_b(z_b^*)z_b^* h(z_b^*).$$

There are two consequences of introducing behavioural agents in this model: an explicit welfare effect and an implicit change in the elasticity. First, the *behavioural wedge* (Bernheim and Taubinsky, 2018) between the MRS of the decision utility and the MRS of the experienced utility has a first-order impact on welfare. For instance, for a given level of consumption and leisure and scaled by the marginal utility from consumption, a workaholic agent can be characterised by a marginal decision disutility from work lower than the marginal experienced disutility – that is, $|v_2/v_1| < |u_2/u_1|$. This agent works too much from the perspective of the experienced utility. Assume for simplicity that agents correctly perceive the tax schedule, such that $T'(z_b) = T'_b(z_b)$. In this case, the bias term is positive: the social planner has a new welfare-related motive to increase taxes in order to bring this person closer to the decisions they would take, were they considering their experienced utility.

Second, the reduced-form elasticity ε_b captures earnings responses according to the decision utility v and taken with respect to a misperceived tax schedule $T_b(z)$: $\varepsilon_b = \frac{\partial z_b}{\partial(1-\tau)}\frac{1-\tau}{z_b}$ at $\tau = T'(z_b)$, the effective marginal tax rate. From a welfare perspective, if these psychological deviations mitigate individual earnings responses, the government can take advantage of this situation to set higher marginal tax rates. In order to gain a better understanding of this formula, assume that (i) tax schedules are linear, such that the perceived linear rate $\tau_b(\tau)$ is a function of the effective linear rate τ, and that (ii) the experienced and decision utilities are quasi-linear with elasticities of taxable income given

---

[18] See Gerritsen (2016) for more insights on the optimal non-linear income tax when the decision utility differs from the experienced utility.

by ε_x and ε_d respectively. In a standard taxation framework, derivation of the first-order condition of the agent's programme with respect to $1 - \tau$ highlights ε_x as a sufficient statistic. With behavioural agents, an empirical estimation provides the reduced-form elasticity: $\varepsilon_b = \varepsilon_d \cdot \varepsilon_{1-\tau_b/1-\tau}$, where $\varepsilon_{1-\tau_b/1-\tau}$ is the elasticity of the perceived net-of-marginal tax rate with respect to the effective net-of-marginal tax rate. If agents correctly perceive the tax schedule, we are able to recover their decision elasticity ε_d. Otherwise, this decision elasticity will be amplified or diminished depending on the way the behavioural agent perceives the tax schedule. As mentioned in the introduction to this section, it could also be that $\varepsilon_{1-\tau_b/1-\tau}$ is low for small variations in tax rates, but much larger for stronger tax reforms. In this case, a reduced-form elasticity measured in a given context may not systematically be applicable to predict the effects of future reforms.

Introducing behavioural agents changes standard optimal tax formulas. Farhi and Gabaix (2020) demonstrate that negative income tax rates may be optimal for low-income taxpayers who underestimate the future benefits from work. When taxpayers are characterised by heterogeneous biases, Bernheim and Taubinsky (2018) find that optimal taxes depend on the correlation between bias and responsiveness to tax incentives.

This theoretical approach raises many questions for empirical investigations. Should we estimate the reduced-form elasticity ε_b or try to reach a structural elasticity? Under which assumptions is it possible to disentangle this structural elasticity from behavioural biases? Do we need to estimate this bias for welfare analysis?

Sales Taxes

A behavioural agent with decision utility v will consume x_b such that $v'(x_b) = p + \tau$. However, the government who considers their experienced utility still maximises welfare according to Equation (2). The welfare impact of a small increase in the sales tax is given by:

$$\frac{dW}{d\tau} = \tau \frac{dx_b}{d\tau} + \left(u'(x_b) - (p + \tau)\right)\frac{dx_b}{d\tau} = \tau \frac{dx_b}{d\tau} + \underbrace{\left(u'(x_b) - v'(x_b)\right)}_{\substack{behavioural \\ wedge}} \frac{dx_b}{d\tau}$$

$$= (\tau - b)\frac{dx_b}{d\tau}. \tag{4}$$

The *behavioural wedge* b captures the discrepancy between the marginal decision and experienced utilities. If the social planner implements another tax equal to this behavioural wedge $t = b$, then the behavioural agent will choose consumption x^*, such that $v'(x^*) = p + \tau + t$, which is maximising their experienced utility since $p + \tau = u'(x^*)$. As explained by Bernheim and Taubinsky (2018), this new tax *prices out the bias*: it brings the behavioural agent back to the decision of a traditional agent.

To develop understanding, consider the theoretical framework developed by Chetty et al. (2009) to analyse the behavioural responses they measured in their in-store experiment, presented in Section 3.1.3. Behavioural consumers take their decisions with respect to their experienced utility u but perceive the tax rate τ as if it were equal to $\tau_b = \theta \tau$. The authors estimate $\theta = 0.35$, which means that consumers react to sales taxes as if they were equal to only 35 per cent of their true value. These agents consume x_b, such that $u'(x_b) = p + \theta \tau$. Plugging this expression in Equation (4), we have:

$$\frac{dW}{d\tau} = \theta \tau \frac{dx_b}{d\tau}. \tag{5}$$

This expression is nearly identical to the standard Harberger triangle. Marginal welfare consequences of tax rate variations are dampened or exacerbated depending on whether behavioural agents underestimate ($\theta < 1$) or overestimate ($\theta > 1$) the tax rate, since they perceive a smaller tax increase in the former case and a bigger one in the latter case.

Figure 2 illustrates the impact of limited attention on the deadweight loss of sales taxes highlighted by Chetty et al. (2009) for a fixed producer price p_0. The demand of a fully attentive agent $x(p_0 + \tau)$ is determined by the tax-inclusive price, such that $u'(x(p_0 + \tau)) = p_0 + \tau$. As a sales tax τ is implemented, they adjust their consumption downward from x_0 to x_1, which results in a deadweight loss equal to the area of the grey triangle $\left(\frac{\tau^2}{2}\frac{dx}{d\tau}\right)$. The demand of a partially attentive agent ($\theta < 1$) faced with sales taxes τ is given by $x_b(p_0, \tau) = x(p_0 + \theta \tau)$. Without taxes, this agent consumes the same quantity x_0 as an unbiased agent, under the assumption that biases do not apply to prices. For this behavioural agent, limited attention implies lower consumption responses $x_b - x_0$, which results in a smaller deadweight loss equal to $\theta \frac{\tau^2}{2}\frac{dx}{d\tau}$.

From an empirical perspective, wrongly assuming unbiased agents would lead to biased elasticity, since earnings responses would be related to variations in tax rates without accounting for the part of these responses resulting from behavioural biases. Such elasticities would not be very informative for policy recommendations since they would be subject to framing effects purely altering the magnitude of the bias.

A major consequence of salience is that, contrary to standard PF, the effective incidence of taxes on behavioural agents depends on their statutory incidence, which could explain the difference in magnitude between the responses to

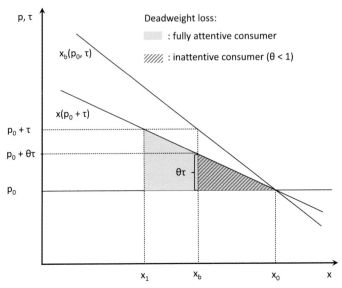

Figure 2 Deadweight loss from sales taxes with limited attention
Note: This figure replicates the graphical presentation of the deadweight loss from sales taxes with limited attention in Chetty et al. (2009). The demand of a standard fully attentive agent $x(p_0 + \tau)$ and the demand of a partially inattentive agent $x_b(p_0, \tau)$ are expressed as a function of a fixed producer price p_0 and a sales tax rate τ.

different taxes. On French data, Lehmann et al. (2013) estimate a positive elasticity of labour income with respect to the income tax, which was very salient at the time. In contrast, they find that workers do not react to variations in payroll taxes, which are much less salient than income taxes since they are not included in the net wage.[19]

3.2.3 Unemployment Insurance and Job Search Behaviour

An unemployed worker may misevaluate their utility from employment, for instance because they are subject to a projection bias or have a strong preference for the present. Assuming that this worker is not biased with respect to their current unemployment situation, their decision utility is given by $v(c_e) \neq u(c_e)$ and $\forall B, v(B) = u(B)$. They choose the level of effort e_b, such

---

[19] Another widely discussed topic in behavioural public finance is the taxation of internalities (Bernheim and Taubinsky, 2018; Farhi and Gabaix, 2020). In this case, behavioural biases provide a new argument in favour of higher taxes. Even though taxes on cigarettes (Gruber and Kőszegi, 2004) or soda (Allcott et al., 2019) are mostly borne by low-income consumers, they can be optimal in order to offset internalities, for instance by providing a self-control mechanism for time-inconsistent consumers.

that $\psi'(e_b) = v(c_e) - u(B)$. The welfare impact of unemployment benefits now features a new term resulting from this behavioural bias:

$$\frac{1 + D}{D}\frac{dW}{dB} = u'_u - u'_e - \varepsilon_{b,D}u'_e - \frac{\varepsilon_{b,D}}{B(1 + D)}\underbrace{(u(c_e) - v(c_e))}_{behavioural\ wedge}, \tag{6}$$

where the elasticity $\varepsilon_{b,D}$ encompasses the consequences of the behavioural bias on the duration of unemployment. A behavioural agent who underestimates the value from employment has an additional motive to remain unemployed. This bias would exacerbate the impact of benefits on unemployment duration, which provides a rationale for lower unemployment benefits.

Traditionally, the labour supply of unemployed workers depends on their reservation wage (e.g. the wage for their previous job), for which they are indifferent between taking a job offer or remaining unemployed. In this case, their decision utility features a reference point,[20] which can be represented according to the functional specification developed by Köszegi and Rabin (2006):

$$v(w - \tau) = u(w - \tau) + \eta(u(w - \tau) - u(w^r))\left[1 + (\lambda - 1)I_{\{w - \tau < w^r\}}\right],$$

wherein w^r is their (net) reference wage. The gain–loss utility component exists if $\eta > 0$, in which case this agent displays loss aversion if $\lambda > 1$: marginal utility is higher below the reference wage than above this level. Empirically, DellaVigna et al. (2022) surveyed 6,800 UI recipients twice a week for four months and found that the pattern of job-search effort over the unemployment spell is consistent with such reference-dependent preferences. Plugging this functional specification for reference dependence in Equation 6, we have:

$$\frac{1 + D}{D}\frac{dW}{dB} = u'_u - u'_e - \varepsilon_{b,D}u'_e$$

$$+ \frac{\varepsilon_{b,D}}{B(1 + D)}\eta(u(w - \tau) - u(w^r))[1 + (\lambda - 1)I_{\{w - \tau < w^r\}}].$$

In the gain domain ($w - \tau \geq w^r$), finding a new job provides an increment of utility to this behavioural agent, which justifies higher unemployment benefits. In contrast, in the loss domain, this agent would suffer from getting a job below their expectations, and even more so in the case of strong loss aversion ($\lambda \gg 1$). Measuring reference wages, the difference between reference and re-entry wages, the magnitude of loss aversion and the correlations between these

---

[20] In a more complex but also more realistic setting, DellaVigna et al. (2017) show that an adaptive reference point outperforms a large array of standard job search models to account for the spike in the hazard rate upon benefits exhaustion. Section 4 discusses this paper in details.

quantities would help in quantifying the aggregate incidence of reference-dependent preferences on optimal unemployment benefits.

Behavioural biases play an important role in the determination of optimal UI benefits. With standard agents, optimal unemployment benefits decrease over the unemployment spell in order to provide increasing incentives over time to search for a new job (Hopenhayn and Nicolini, 1997). In contrast, when unemployed workers are over-optimistic about their employment prospects, Spinnewijn (2015) shows that they do not search actively for a new job and that increasing benefits can be optimal. Using a survey to elicit job-seekers' perception of their employment prospects, Mueller et al. (2021) confirm that over-optimistic unemployed workers are less likely to find a job quickly and do not revise their beliefs over the unemployment spell. In line with limited attention to future income changes, Ganong and Noel (2019) observe that non-durable spending drops sharply upon job loss and benefits exhaustion, but remains stable during UI receipt. They conclude that extending the duration of UI benefits would generate larger consumption-smoothing welfare gains than increasing the level of benefits.[21]

3.2.4 Selection into Health Insurance Programmes

In standard public economics, health insurance programmes are designed in order to deal with information asymmetries (Rothschild and Stiglitz, 1976). It is assumed that agents know their health level, are able to forecast their probabilities of sickness and understand the features of health insurance. Insurers do not observe private information about individual health. They design health plans in order to prevent the sole enrolment of individuals with poor health (adverse selection) or the overuse of medical care (moral hazard) which could generate both financial deficits and welfare losses.

In contrast, empirical investigations reveal that people appear quite bad at evaluating their own health status, at committing to a medical treatment over time, at predicting low-probability diseases or at understanding deductibles. Health insurance policyholders may overuse medical care due to a poor diet or failure to exercise rather than just because they are insured (Congdon et al., 2011). Overconfident agents who underestimate their risks of sickness may underinsure (Sandroni and Squintani, 2007). Subject to projection biases, individuals place too much weight on the current state in their decision process when buying or cancelling health insurance coverage (Chang et al., 2018).

---

[21] For further developments on behavioural labour economics, see Fehr et al. (2009); Babcock et al. (2012); Dohmen (2014).

These psychological deviations influence the optimal design of health insurance policies. According to the standard health insurance theory, the demand elasticity is a sufficient statistic for the design of health insurance. Agents who are very responsive to the price of a treatment would derive a low value from it, so a high demand elasticity would signal overconsumption and call for higher co-payments. When misuse of healthcare is related to psychological deviations, Baicker et al. (2015) explain that this elasticity is not sufficient to derive welfare analysis, as behavioural biases can offset the effect of moral hazard. For example, self-control issues may lead agents to consume too little health care. Moreover, when faced with behavioural agents, the principal gains an informational advantage. Private health insurers could exploit individual biases to sell dominated health coverage to pessimistic people with a high cognitive load. Considering behavioural biases in PF provides a new reason for the development of public rather than private insurance.[22]

3.3 Do We Need to Specify Behavioural Biases?

The former examples presented two ways to include psychological deviations in PF models. On the one hand, many biases can be represented as a behavioural wedge between marginal rates of substitution. On the other hand, building on BE models, biases can be expressed using structural parameters (inattention θ, hyperbolic discounting factor β, loss aversion λ, etc.). As discussed in Kleven (2021), this debate between structural models and sufficient statistics is quite central in PF. Which approach should we favour?

3.3.1 When is a Behavioural Model Really Needed?

The sufficient statistics approach is convenient because the behavioural wedge can generally encompass a wide range of biases,[23] so we do not need to take a stand on the exact bias in order to assess the welfare consequences of a reform. To combat a negative externality, the government wants to discourage some behaviours independently from their psychological nature. Its goal is to determine the level of transfers that leads agents to internalise the externality. Provided that fiscal reforms do not involve framing effects which could not be encompassed in behavioural elasticities, the sufficient statistics approach will be favoured in such cases as it does not require any assumption regarding

---

[22] For developments in behavioural health care, see Frank (2012); Rice (2013); Chandra et al. (2019).

[23] As stated by Chetty et al. (2009) (p. 1148): 'Although we motivate our welfare analysis by evidence of salience effects, the formulas account for all errors that consumers may make when optimizing with respect to taxes.'

the shape of preferences or potential biases. However, as discussed in Section 3.2, sufficient statistics should be estimated with caution since they embed behavioural adjustments.

Structural estimations require a lot of information in order to estimate each parameter of a model, whether behavioural or not, but prove very powerful for out-of-sample predictions and comparisons with the literature in BE. When public policies alter frames, they can activate some behavioural biases and therefore trigger hardly expectable individual responses. Explicitly modelling behavioural biases can be very helpful in reducing this unpredictable component. As developed in Kleven and Kopczuk (2011), the welfare consequence of policies improving the take-up of social benefits depends on whether such policies efficiently address the reasons why the neediest households fail to claim these benefits in the first place (administrative costs, lack of information, behavioural biases, etc.). In this case, a structural model is useful to isolate specific biases, to confront theoretical predictions with empirical observations and, ideally, to reject alternative explanations.

3.3.2 Behavioural Sufficient Statistics

Rees-Jones and Taubinsky (2018) highlight the limits of the mechanism design approach to optimal income taxation when taxpayers are behavioural and they call for a behavioural extension of the sufficient statistics approach. According to the mechanism design methodology presented in the previous section, what matters for the optimal tax is only the choice set of consumption and earnings pairs available to taxpayers and not the type of tax schedule that implements this choice set. This assumption does not hold when agents misperceive the tax schedule, in which case the mechanism design approach may not be informative about welfare, the optimal allocation may not be feasible and adverse selection may be a much less important issue.

Including behavioural agents in non-linear income tax models, Farhi and Gabaix (2020) show that the optimal income tax formula features a new sufficient statistic, which they call the *behavioural cross-influence*, defined as 'the elasticity of the earnings of an agent at earning z to the marginal retention rate $1 - T'(z^*)$ at income $z^* \neq z$'. This elasticity captures earnings responses to normatively irrelevant incentives, such as infra-marginal tax rates. In standard models, this behavioural statistic is always equal to zero. In behavioural models, this elasticity provides a new rational for lower tax rates since, beyond well-known adjustments, increasing the marginal tax rate at one point of the tax schedule would lead agents at other income levels to reduce their labour supply. Lardeux (2021) finds evidence of a significantly positive behavioural cross-influence at the starting point of the French income tax. Tax filers who neglect a tax collection minimum perceive a shadow tax bracket below the earnings level where tax liabilities start. The behavioural cross-influence is dynamically identified on tax filers relocating to the lower bound of this shadow bracket following a rise in the associated perceived marginal tax rate.

4 From Theory to Empirics: Recovering Behavioural Deviations

Behavioural models of PF enable welfare analysis of fiscal policies accounting for psychological deviations. For this purpose, we need to feed the theoretical model with empirical estimates that capture behavioural responses. As is usual in applied microeconomics, this empirical stage proceeds in three steps: identification, data selection and estimation.

The identification step matches each behavioural parameter of the theoretical model with the empirical behavioural deviations it triggers. For a given economic environment, such behavioural deviations can be revealed by choices under different *frames* or optimisation mistakes, but a standard economic model should not be able to provide a rationale for them.

This first step guides the selection of a relevant dataset generated by experiments, surveys or administrations. Each method has its own advantages: experiments allow precise control of the nature and intensity of the treatment; surveys enable the measurement of expectations, beliefs, social preferences or knowledge; and administrative data can be used in quasi-experimental frameworks to validate theories in real-life situations.

The final estimation step consists in retrieving identified behavioural parameters from this dataset. In line with Sections 2 and 3, estimates can be structural or reduced-form parameters. The structural approach fosters extrapolation, while sufficient statistics can deal with (relative) model indeterminacy and be directly recovered through reduced-form causal estimations.

4.1 Identification of Behavioural Deviations

Assessing fiscal reform in PF with behavioural agents requires a cautious identification of behavioural parameters. We have to foresee the observable dimensions needed in order to recover individual behaviours, to make sure that they provide enough information to identify each parameter of the theoretical model and that they could not have been generated by a standard (non-behavioural) economic model. Before that, a graphical approach provides insights into the conditions for proper identification of behavioural parameters.

Graphic elements are often convincing preliminary evidence of identification. They help understand which dimensions of the data are needed and which parameters will ultimately be estimable. This section takes the example of *bunching* methods, which originally came from PF but have new spread widely in BE, as explained by Kleven (2016).

Bunching methods were initially developed by Saez (2010) and Kleven and Waseem (2013) in order to estimate behavioural responses to tax incentives. As stressed by Saez et al. (2012), previous estimation methods required many assumptions and controls in order to deal with endogeneity issues between taxable income and tax rates as well as mean reversion in earnings dynamics. The bunching approach provides a visually convincing alternative.

The left panel of Figure 3 illustrates the identification of behavioural responses from bunching at *kink* points developed by Saez (2010). When faced with a local discontinuity in the income tax schedule which takes the form of a discrete jump $d\tau$ in the marginal tax rate (a *kink*), optimising taxpayers with earnings between z^* and $z^* + dz^*$ have an incentive to reduce their reported earnings in order to locate at this kink. Saez (2010) first showed that the bunching mass in the taxable income distribution at this threshold can be related to the magnitude of the local change in tax incentives in order to identify an elasticity of taxable income. Kleven and Waseem (2013) extended this methodology to discontinuities in average tax rates or *notches*.

Beyond the field of taxation, bunching methods have spread in BE due to their ability to provide convincing graphical evidence of behavioural deviations, especially near reference points. As explained in Section 3, indifference curves of loss-averse agents feature a kink at the reference point related to a discontinuous change in their marginal utility, which provides a rationale to locate there. As depicted by the right panel of Figure 3, it is possible for loss-averse agents to locate in the continuous part of their indifference curves. If we observe individual choices under sufficiently wide variations in the slope of the budget set, then we may be able to identify the magnitude of loss aversion (what DellaVigna (2018) calls 'pricing-out the bias'; see Section 4.1.2). Rees-Jones (2017) presents evidence of a reference point at zero in the balance due on tax day. Loss-averse taxpayers are much more likely to search for tax deductions when they owe money to the tax authority than when they should receive money. Seibold (2021) relies on bunching analysis to show that retirement decisions are mostly related to statutory ages rather than financial incentives.

Bunching more broadly helps in relating individual choices to behavioural biases, mental costs or lack of information. For instance, Chetty et al. (2013) use

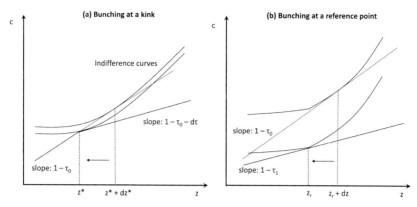

Figure 3 Bunching identification

Note: *Panel (a):* After the introduction of a kink at z^*, the marginal buncher initially located at earnings $z^* + dz^*$ has an incentive to adjust their taxable income in order to relocate at z^*. Since all taxpayers whose earnings were initially between z^* and $z^* + dz^*$ face the same incentive, the variation $d\tau$ in the slope of the budget set generates a bunching mass at z^*. *Panel (b):* with a linear budget set, a bunching mass may occur at an earnings level of reference z_r.

bunching masses as an instrument for the knowledge of fiscal rules in order to estimate an elasticity of labour supply.

Looking at behavioural responses to the threshold where French income tax liabilities start, Lardeux (2021) finds evidence of significant and persistent bunching at an irrelevant Taxation Threshold (TT). As displayed in Figure 4, tax filers who neglect a generalised tax credit appear to perceive a shadow tax bracket just below the effective starting point of the income tax and locate at the resulting kink.

As striking as this pattern is, it is not sufficient to reject a focal point and conclude in favour of tax misperceptions. We need to show that variations in the perceived tax schedule causally trigger earnings responses. For this purpose, the author takes advantage of the panel dimension of the data and shows that the 2012 rise in the marginal tax rate of the shadow bracket induced a significant relocation of tax filers from the effective Tax Collection Threshold (TCT) toward the irrelevant TT. This pattern confirms tax misperceptions and provides a significantly positive estimate for the behavioural cross-influence of the irrelevant threshold.

Figure 5 illustrates this dynamic adjustment. In order to keep a flexible representation for tax misperceptions, the author assumes that each tax filer assigns a weight θ to the effective tax schedule and a weight $1 - \theta$ to the shadow tax bracket. In line with Figure 4, as long as $0 < \theta < 1$, the piecewise linear budget constraint features a kink at the irrelevant TT and a notch at the effective TCT. Following a rise in the marginal tax rate of the shadow bracket, a tax filer

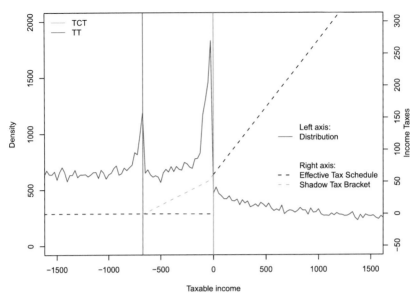

Figure 4 Bunching at an irrelevant Taxation Threshold

Note: This figure is taken from Lardeux (2021). The distribution of taxable income per 25 € bins is depicted on the left axis. The right axis displays the effective income tax schedule, which features a *notch* at the Tax Collection Threshold (TCT), and the shadow tax bracket, which generates a *kink* at the irrelevant Taxation Threshold (TT).

initially at the TCT may relocate to the TT provided that θ is low enough. Under a parametric assumption for the distribution of weights θ, we can infer the mean and variance of tax misperceptions from the share of relocations in 2012. It is worth noting that, even though they misperceive the tax schedule, tax filers are rational since they react to the tax incentives they perceive in the same way as a standard agent would do if those incentives were real.

To sum up, a graphic approach reveals that a standard model cannot account for some behavioural responses, but, in this case, such static evidence is not sufficient to discriminate between different behavioural explanations. Concluding in favour of tax misperceptions requires intra-individual variations in order to observe individual relocations following a tax reform (*natural experiment*). The bunching approach enables a causal estimation, but the identification of the dispersion of tax misperceptions among tax filers requires further parametric assumptions.

4.1.2 Thinking Ahead About Observational Requirements

Identification is a central step in presenting the conditions under which the parameters of a model can be inferred from the data. In a transparent

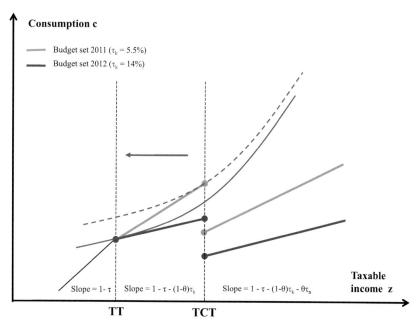

Figure 5 Relocation from the effective to the irrelevant threshold
Note: This figure is taken from Lardeux (2021). Following a rise in the marginal tax rate τ_k of the shadow tax bracket, behavioural tax filers initially at the TCT have an incentive to relocate to the irrelevant TT.

identification stage, each estimator can be expressed as a function of empirical moments. Before diving into econometric analysis, looking at the data and anticipating on required information can be a significant time saver.

Choices under Different Frames

With behavioural agents, identification is even more delicate as individual decisions depend not only on objective economic variables (prices and revenue) but also on the way economic choices are *framed*. A behavioural decision-maker faced with the same choice set will make different decisions depending on whether alternatives are framed as gains or losses, grouped or separated, salient or opaque, etc. In a large-scale experiment on financial incentives for retirement saving contributions, Saez (2009) found that the take-up of a subsidy is much higher when it is framed as a 50 per cent matching contribution rather than a 33 per cent credit rebate, even though both policies are strictly equivalent.

Ideally, in order to recover the influence of the bias on individual decisions, we would need to observe the same choice under a biased frame and a debiased frame. This debiased frame is defined such that, under this frame, the behavioural agent makes the same decisions as a standard economic agent. For instance, as discussed in Section 3.1.3, Chetty et al. (2009) design their experiment such that they observe consumption decisions in grocery stores when only pre-tax prices are displayed, such that consumers may neglect sales taxes (biased frame) and when price tags display tax-inclusive prices (debiased frame).

Of course, this identification relies on the assumption that agents can be fully debiased, which cannot be verified in practice. The experimenter may add a complementary questionnaire in order to ensure that subjects are informed about their decision environment and understand the underlying mechanisms as well as the consequences of their choices. Yet, there is no guarantee that the agent makes their decision based on their experienced utility. Beyond this empirical aspect of identification, taking the debiased frame as a normative reference for fiscal policy design is not self-evident. We return to this question in the final section.

Taking Advantage of Intra-Individual Variations

Using multiple observations for the same individual is usually an efficient way to recover preferences. Under the WARP and an assumption of preferences stability, these preferences can often be identified from individual adjustments to price changes. In a standard model, this is an efficient way to estimate structural parameters such as risk aversion, time-discounting factors or elasticities. In behavioural models, DellaVigna (2018) highlights a useful aspect of this methodology to *price-out the bias*. Price variations can be used in an experiment to estimate some common structural parameters, such as the discount factor δ, while significant behavioural departures from the predictions of a standard model can be related to psychological biases, such as the present-bias parameter β in a hyperbolic preferences or $\beta\delta$ model. Even though it is not the parameter of interest, estimation of a discount factor is mandatory to recover the bias and express it in monetary terms. In BPF, such an estimation of incidental parameters is key to relate biases to taxes and transfers.

Similarly, biases could be identified from changes in frames holding the economic environment constant. Since frames do not impact preferences, any change in behaviour can be attributed to a behavioural bias and intra-individual variations can efficiently separate biases from preferences. Data with multiple observations of the same individual observed under different frames are not commonplace but can be collected in an experiment, as in the article by Allcott and Taubinsky (2015) that is presented in detail in Section 4.3.2. An additional reward of this approach is the ability to analyse bias heterogeneity among the sample of interest.

Laying Outside the Identification Domain

A general remark on the revealed-preferences methodology is that preferences are empirically identified only among agents who modify their choice for some value of the vector of prices. When individual decisions are only observed for discrete values on a given range of relative prices, preference parameters of subjects who stick to the same choice can be bounded but not point-identified. Similarly, behavioural biases are measured by the relative magnitude of behavioural agents' adjustments compared with welfare-relevant adjustments by agents with similar preferences in the same economic environment. Lack of adjustment is not proof of behavioural biases. A consumer whose willingness to pay is always below or above an offered price will never or always buy this good, respectively. Empirically, we are only able to bound their willingness to pay and cannot conclude any bias on their part just from this lack of adjustment.

Looking for Mistakes

Psychological deviations matter for PF when they trigger unexpected behavioural responses. Following a backward approach, we can rely on the identification of individual mistakes in order to recover behavioural biases. Of course, this approach assumes that the analyst is able to characterise some choices as mistakes and to distinguish them from the expression of singular preferences. We discuss this assumption in the final section.

Some dominated choices can undoubtedly be classified as mistakes since they lead to sub-optimal allocations, regardless of individual preferences. Looking at decisions from nearly 24,000 employees at a US firm, Bhargava et al. (2017) found that more than half of them opted for a dominated health plan with low deductible and high premiums. In this paper, a health plan is dominated by another if, regardless of the level of medical expenses, the latter would be less expensive for the employee than the former. Importantly, the choice of a dominated plan cannot be simply rationalised by plan complexity. Whether subjects are presented with menus characterised by few or many plans, the propensity to choose a dominated plan stays the same. However, this choice is much less prevalent among subjects with a higher insurance literacy and is strongly reduced when the financial implications of each plan are simplified and compared with each other. A nice feature of this natural experiment is that employees were informed about health plans since they could build their own plan as a combination of several components.

In the absence of dominated choices, mistakes can be revealed by irrelevant choices from the perspective of a standard economic agent. Feldman et al. (2016) studied the behavioural responses of American households who lost the benefits from the CTC when their child turned seventeen. Such a rise in lump-sum taxes should not distort the trade-off between consumption and leisure or even slightly stimulate labour supply through income effect. However, they observed a significant drop in labour supply, which they relate to a confusion between lump-sum and marginal taxes. Taxpayers interpret a rise in lump-sum taxes as an increase in their marginal tax rate and rationally adjust their labour supply downward.

4.1.3 Pitfalls of Identification and How to Prevent Them

Positive evidence of psychological deviation requires not only observing imperfect optimisation, but also ensuring that it cannot be explained by standard economic mechanisms such as regulatory constraints, adjustment costs or lack of information. Before the estimation stage, a primary investigation of the data may provide insights about the model behind unexpected observed choices.

Alternative Non-Behavioural Explanations

On top of their main experiment presented in Section 3.1.3, in order to identify limited attention, Chetty et al. (2009) compared the impacts of sales taxes and excise taxes on beer consumption. Excise taxes should be more salient than sales taxes since they are included in posted prices. The authors found that the elasticity of demand with respect to the excise tax is much stronger than the elasticity with respect to the sales tax. However, the tax base of the sales tax includes a much broader set of goods than just alcoholic beverages, since 40 per cent of consumption goods are subject to sales taxes. The discrepancy between the two elasticities could therefore be the consequence of different distortive impacts of these two taxes on alcohol consumption compared to other consumption goods. In order to discard this alternative explanation, the authors developed two tests. First, they estimate similar elasticities in states that fully exempt food items from the sales tax, such that both taxes have the same distortive impact. Second, through a calibration exercise they show that, even if we take the largest estimated response to the sales tax, price distortions induced by a rise in alcohol taxes cannot account for the difference between the two elasticities. Standard tax theory cannot account for the dampened response to the sales tax.

In contrast, Benzarti (2017) explains that the non-negligible share of American taxpayers who do not itemise their deductions can be rationalised in a standard model with administrative costs (record-keeping, cognitive load, understanding fiscal rules, etc.). Saez (2010) shows evidence of behavioural responses to changes in marginal tax rates in the form of a bunching mass at the threshold where income tax liabilities start. However, this mass appears only among self-employed workers and not among wage earners, presumably because the latter cannot adjust their reported earnings as easily as the former.

Behavioural Bias or Lack of Information?

Just because people have access to free information does not mean that they take it into account when making decisions. Even in an environment with full information, behavioural agents may be subject to biases. In order to prove that these biases are truly identified, empirical papers in BPF take great care to discuss the knowledge of and information available to individual decision-makers. While measuring demand responses to tax-inclusive price tags, Chetty et al. (2009) surveyed grocery shoppers and showed that, most of the time, despite their limited attention, subjects know the applicable tax rate. The theoretical counterpart is that the expression of behavioural biases goes beyond a simple lack of information and could not be rationalised in a standard model with incomplete information.

This distinction between biased choices and lack of information matters for policy design. A one-shot intervention can be sufficient to permanently inform a previously uninformed agent, whereas it can be less effective for behavioural agents who already have this knowledge but neglect it when making choices. Using a natural experiment, Boutchenik and Lardeux (2020) illustrate the separation between information frictions and behavioural deviations among unemployed workers. They study a mailing sent to unemployed workers near benefits exhaustion, which indicates their potential eligibility to unemployment benefit extensions. This letter mentions that, in order to apply for such an extension, claimants should certificate each job taken since the beginning of their current spell. Following the implementation of this reform, claimants ended up with an additional month of potential benefit duration on average. On the one hand, first-time unemployed workers, who have less experience in the UI system, started certifying their past employment history. On the other hand, claimants in their second, third or fourth unemployment spell, and therefore arguably more experienced but still subject to the cognitive load of unemployment, used to miss certifying some jobs. Once the mailing was implemented, they started certifying their past jobs much more systematically. The same instrument acts as an information provision on the former and a reminder on the latter.

Handel and Schwartzstein (2018) argue that identification of the reasons why agents do not use freely available information is essential when the effectiveness of public policies depends on the context in which they are implemented (information provision, framing, reminders). When information processing involves a costly friction, the social planner may consider the limited take-up of benefits as the result of a cost–benefit analysis from an agent allocating mental resources to different activities. In contrast, investigating the correlation between behavioural biases and earnings is essential if incomplete take-up is related to cognitive difficulties from someone actively trying to claim benefits. These two cases should display very different correlations between individual choices and earnings.

4.2 Which Data?

With these identification requirements in mind, we can consider the most appropriate sources of information among experiments, administrative data and surveys. Experiments ensure a strong internal consistency since the experimenter can randomise the assignment to the control and treatment groups and precisely adjust the nature and intensity of the treatment. Fiscal reforms investigated using administrative data often provide quasi-experimental frameworks with a strong external validity since they are based on real-life decisions. Surveys are a powerful way to collect information about expectations, beliefs, social preferences and knowledge.

4.2.1 Experiments in Public Finance

Experiments are a powerful way to manipulate frames in order to precisely identify behavioural biases. Individual actions can be measured under different frames inducing deviations from what would be expected from a standard economic agent. A long-lasting research tradition in behavioural and experimental economics discusses the conditions under which inference about individual behaviour can be conducted in experiments. Through a few examples, this section illustrates how useful they can be to improve our understanding of individual behavioural responses in PF. For deeper insight into experimental economics, readers may refer to: Kagel and Roth (1995); Durlauf and Blume (2009); Bardsley et al. (2010); Banerjee and Duflo (2017); and Jacquemet and L'Haridon (2018).

Lab Experiments

Public finance regularly stresses a lack of responses with respect to non-negligible incentives: why do people seem not to optimise? Abeler and Jäger (2015) conducted an experiment wherein subjects worked for a piece rate and were taxed. One group faced a simple version of a tax schedule and the other a complex version with almost identical tax incentives but many more rules (twenty-two, against two in the simple treatment). Then they introduced the same new incentive, which changes the payoff-maximising output level, in the tax schedules of the two groups. They observed that optimisation is much stronger in the first group, with respect to both the baseline payoff-maximising output level and to this new rule. In a complex system, subjects are less able to find the payoff-maximising output level and less responsive to tax reforms. It would be difficult to find a real-life framework enabling such a causal inference about the impact of complexity on decision-making. In such cases, lab experiments prove extremely valuable.

Field Experiments

Field experiments are a popular tool in PF to test the impact of an intervention on a small sample of the population. The experimenter designs a causal evaluation framework wherein participants are randomly assigned to either a treatment or a control group. Agents evolve in a real economic environment altered only at the margin by the experimenter. Informational interventions appear as a powerful way to test different frames and reveal biases in action.

Consider the incomplete take-up of social benefits, which has been widely documented in many countries. As highlighted by Currie (2006), eligible household fail to take up social benefits due to transaction costs, stigma or lack of information. Behavioural biases such as procrastination, limited attention, inaccurate beliefs, loss aversion in case of undue payments or cognitive load may also be responsible for limited take-up (Mullainathan et al., 2012; Mullainathan and Shafir, 2013). An efficient allocation of social benefits requires a better understanding of the channels preventing full take-up. Teleprocessing may reduce transportation costs, a simple reminder can act effectively against procrastination or imperfect salience, whereas assistance may be required when people do not understand the system at all.

In order to identify the origins of incomplete take-up of EITC benefits, Bhargava and Manoli (2015) randomly distributed experimental mailings to 35,000 American tax filers who failed to claim this tax credit. They conceived different versions of the same notice, each one framing the recipient in a different way: a simplified notice summarises the most relevant features to address administrative complexity, a high-salience notice highlights the refund the recipient might be eligible to, a transaction-cost notice presents the time it usually takes to fill out the claiming worksheet and a notice aimed at reducing stigma mentions that the recipient 'will not be penalised for unintended errors'. In this case, the first two versions substantially increased refund claiming while the others did not, suggesting that the incomplete take-up of EITC benefits is mostly related to administrative complexity, low understanding and lack of salience. Moreover, they find that simplification mostly helped low earners. A complementary survey confirmed that this intervention changed beliefs about eligibility and benefits and drew attention to administrative forms.

The take-up of social benefits cannot be easily measured in administrative data, since non-takers are generally missing. In this case, a field experiment is a powerful solution to measure take-up rates among a sample of likely eligible individuals and estimate the impact of several interventions on take-up. Finkelstein and Notowidigdo (2019) designed a randomised field experiment in order to analyse the take-up of the Supplemental Nutrition Assistance Program (SNAP) among 30,000 eligible elderly Americans. SNAP is the second-largest means-tested programme in the US, and provides food-purchasing benefits for low-income households. A mailing informed households in the treatment group about their eligibility to SNAP and they received a follow-up reminder. On top of that, some of them benefited from application assistance. Nine months after the intervention, 6 per cent of the control group joined the SNAP programme, as well as 11 per cent of those who only received the mailing and 18 per cent of those who benefited from information and assistance. Overall, the authors interpret their results as evidence of benefits underestimation and limited attention, since they note a lower impact of the information treatment without a reminder.

Lab-in-the-Field Experiments

Between lab and field experiments, a continuum of lab-in-the-field experiments combine the two approaches in order to replicate the precision of experimenter control in a naturalistic setting. They build on both the internal validity of laboratory experiments and the external validity of field experiments. Gneezy and Imas (2017) define lab-in-the-field studies as experiments 'conducted in a naturalistic environment targeting the theoretically relevant population but using a standardised, validated lab paradigm'. They are generally performed to elicit the decision process of a representative sample of the population or an informed group relevant for an economic behaviour of interest.

Lab-in-the-field experiments are particularly relevant to analyse online consumption decisions, as they make it feasible to recreate and manipulate a virtual shopping environment. Taubinsky and Rees-Jones (2018) developed an online lab-in-the-field experiment in order to evaluate the welfare consequences of limited attention to sales taxes. They elicited the willingness to pay for common consumption products among a sample of 3,000 subjects representative of the population from the forty-five US states with positive sales taxes. Each individual was asked to state the price at which they would buy an item under three incentive-compatible decision environments (*frames*): no sales tax, the sales tax of their city of residence and three times this sales tax. In order to identify a level of attention, consumers were not told the tax rate that applies in their city of residence and the no-tax treatment emphasised the absence of taxes. The results were computed among informed subjects who understand how to compute sales taxes, and the authors show that most of them know precisely the sales tax rate in their city of residence. Comparing willingness to pay with and without taxes, the authors first estimate that consumers display an average degree of attention of 0.25 to sales taxes: when making purchasing decisions, they take into account the sales tax rate as if it were only equal to a quarter of its effective value. More interestingly, using within-individual variations in tax rates, these authors estimate that consumers take into account nearly half of sales taxes when the tax rate is multiplied by three. Hence, they are able to show that attention is endogenous: consumers pay more attention when sales taxes stand for a higher share of the price. In this paper, the control over the design of the experiment enables the observation of choices under different frames for the same individual. At the same time, using a representative sample ensures that welfare conclusions can be generalised.

4.2.2 Administrative Data and Natural Experiments

Developments in administrative data reached new heights in the past decade. Administrations rely increasingly on centralised information systems collecting data automatically and instantaneously. Detailed households finances can be recovered from linked tax returns, employer statements, bank accounts, social security and social welfare benefits. On the downside, estimates may be impacted by a selection problem if households who do not fill out a tax return are missing. Furthermore, administrative data only gather information useful for the computation of public transfers, while essential household characteristics from the point of view of the researcher may be left out. Finally, even though most of the time the data-collection process is automated through accountability software of third-party reporting organisations (employer, banks, employment agencies, social security, etc.), some variables, still filled out by tax filers, may be subject to caution since they may be subject to (conscious or unconscious) reporting biases.

Many papers in PF are based on *natural experiments* evaluated using administrative data: the treatment is implemented by a political reform and the assignment to the treatment or the control group is based on some observable characteristics such as age, residence, industry and so on. This setting is arguably the most realistic in terms of both public policy and the individual decision environment. Yet, the researcher has to prove that assignment is as good as random, which may be complicated since reforms are often targeted toward specific populations. A cautious discussion of confounding factors is often mandatory in order to delineate the scope of the results.

Hastings and Shapiro (2018) provide a nice illustration of how administrative sources may reveal mental accounting mechanisms among recipients of the SNAP program. Standard economic theory assumes fungibility of money in the household budget. In contrast, BE find that 'mental accounting matters' (Thaler, 1999). In order to organise their spending and short-term savings, individuals tend to mentally regroup their financial activities by source of earnings (wage, capital income, benefits, etc.) or destination (housing, groceries, energy, holidays, etc.). As stated by Thaler (1999, p. 185), 'Money in one mental account is not a perfect substitute for money in another account.'

In practice, SNAP recipients have a debit card credited each month with the amount of benefits that they can spend on SNAP-eligible groceries (mostly food). According to standard economic theory, when faced with a rise in benefits, households whose food expenditures exceed SNAP benefits should display the same marginal propensity to consume (MPC) out of these benefits and out of cash. This incremental amount of benefits is assumed fungible in their budgets.

In order to estimate the causal impact of SNAP on consumption spending, the authors relied on a monthly panel of purchases from half a million customers in a large US grocery retailer from 2006 to 2012. They take advantage of most of the SNAP rules and reforms in order to levy three distinct estimation approaches: an event study, an instrumental variable (IV) design and a difference-in-differences estimation strategy. First, identification within the event study is based on the trend of household spending around SNAP enrolment. Figure 6 shows monthly expenditure of SNAP-eligible and SNAP-ineligible spendings before and after SNAP adoption. Upon SNAP adoption, sampled households receive approximately $200 of social benefits. They increase SNAP-eligible spending by $110 and SNAP-ineligible spending by only $5, which implies very different MPCs. Second, SNAP enrolment is valid for six months, after which re-certification is required. The authors use this timing of programme exit as an exogenous instrument for the fall in SNAP benefits. Third, the difference-in-differences estimation relies on the comparison of spending between SNAP recipients and comparable non-recipients around two reforms that discretely increased SNAP benefits in October 2008 and April 2009. All three methods converge toward an MPC out of SNAP of between 0.5 and 0.6 and an MPC out of cash of 0.1.

Households treat different sources of income differently: SNAP benefits appear to be mentally assigned to food purchases. Whereas a standard model cannot account for such a difference, a structural model where mental

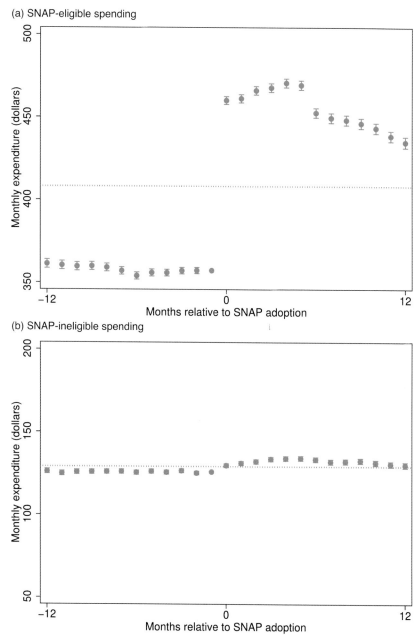

Figure 6 Monthly Expenditure around SNAP Adoption

Note: The dotted lines show the sample mean of household monthly expenditure across observations within twelve months of SNAP adoption.

Source: Hastings, J. and Shapiro, J. M. (2018) How Are SNAP benefits spent? Evidence from a retail panel. *American Economic Review,* 108(12): 3493–540. [Copyright American Economic Association; reproduced with permission of the *American Economic Review*].

accounting takes the form of a linear cost of deviating from a default can. Households are willing to give up 0.84 per cent of monthly consumption in order to avoid the cost of a $100 deviation from their mental account. The authors conclude that SNAP is particularly efficient with mental accounters, since the government can rely on this psychological tendency to provide precise incentives to purchase SNAP food, even when recipients have other sources of income.

4.2.3 Surveys

Survey elicitation is a powerful method to access individual beliefs, representations, perceptions and other mental models of the economy, which is a prerequisite in order to design well-suited fiscal policies (Stantcheva, 2021). Manski (2004) even criticises estimations of decision processes based on revealed preferences on the grounds that they implicitly rely on an assumption of probabilistic expectations and he stands for a direct estimation of subjective probabilities based on survey data.

Of course, survey elicitation has many downsides. First, surveys do not reveal choices. Agents may know certain information but not use it in some contexts (Gabaix, 2019) or intuitively use some relevant features with their fast, automatic and emotional System 1 (Kahneman, 2011) that they would not be able to convey with their more logical and conscious System 2 during a survey. Second, the social interaction with the interviewer may trigger response biases or memory biases. Respondents may feel social pressure to express an opinion or may experience cognitive dissonance (Bertrand and Mullainathan, 2001). Third, answers to the same question generally vary with the ordering of questions in the survey, the ordering of items in a question, the choice of words, the partition of a scale, etc., such that each of these dimensions should ideally be controlled for when analysing the results of a survey.

Keeping these limitations in mind, surveys can be used to elicit individual mental representations of price and tax schedules. Rees-Jones and Taubinsky (2020) asked 4,200 US taxpayers to predict income taxes associated with different levels of income. Nearly half of individual responses did not match the amount that would be computed using the effective tax schedule, but were consistent with the 'ironing' heuristic: taxpayers extrapolated the tax schedule starting from their own income level and using their own average tax rate. The authors showed that their estimation holds for a wide variety of sample restrictions related to the strength of incentives, the ability to fill out taxes without assistance, the level of income and the proximity of tax day. Exploiting households responses to electricity price variations along a non-linear schedule, Ito (2014) find similar evidence that they optimise with respect to the average price instead of the marginal price.

Surveys are also particularly relevant to quantify subjective well-being. A recent literature investigates the use of subjective well-being and happiness data in order to identify individual preferences (Frey and Stutzer, 2002; Di Tella and MacCulloch, 2006; Benjamin et al., 2014). Eliciting subjective well-being is crucial to measure contingent valuation in domains where choices cannot be observed, which often occurs with environmental externalities and public goods, such as the willingness to protect wilderness areas (Carson, 2012).

4.2.4 Using Multiple Sources of Information

Replication of empirical results using different sources of information strengthens the credibility of the estimation. Chetty et al. (2009) show evidence of limited attention using two different sources of information: a field experiment, which is outlined in Section 3.1.3, and aggregate data on alcohol consumption between 1970 and 2003, presented in Section 4.1.3. As discussed in Section 4.3.2, Allcott and Taubinsky (2015) measure the impact of information on purchase of compact fluorescent lightbulbs (CFLs) in a lab experiment and on the field at a home improvement retailer.

Experiments or administrative data enriched with surveys is useful to investigate the sources of specific behaviours. Handel and Kolstad (2015) combined administrative panel data on health plan choices of 50,000 employees from a large US firm with a survey of 4,500 of them to identify the main drivers of insurance plan decisions. They tested subjects' knowledge about financial and non-financial aspects of health plans, recovered their beliefs about their expected medical expenditures and asked them about time and hassle costs of the plan used. The authors conclude that a substantial part of what is generally labelled as risk preferences in revealed-preferences models can actually be related to information frictions and hassle costs.

In some cases, the consequences of behavioural deviations can only be revealed through the joint confrontation of surveys, administrative data and experiments. Interested in the behavioural origins of social preferences, Cruces et al. (2013) asked a sample of 1,100 households representative of the urban area of Buenos Aires about their position in the income distribution and collected their income levels in order to measure their effective position. They found that poorer households tend to overestimate their rank while richer households tend to underestimate it. In order to explain this pattern, the authors postulate an inference bias. Rich households generally live in rich neighbourhoods and poor households in poor neighbourhoods. When households report their own position in the income distribution, they evaluate their rank within their reference group and fail to account for selection into this group. Therefore, compared to their neighbours, poor households feel relatively richer and rich households relatively poorer. Consistently, the authors find that households' perceptions of their relative income is mostly correlated with their rank in the income distribution of their reference group rather than in the whole population. Finally, the authors rely on a debiasing experiment in order to relate this perceived rank to social preferences. They surveyed households about their support for redistributive policies and informed some of them about their effective position. Informed households who used to overestimate their position support redistributive policies more often.

4.3 Estimation of Behavioural Models

Once behavioural responses are identified, estimates of their sign, size and dispersion are insightful for policy design. A structural approach proves very useful when the researcher has a strong belief in a specific model of behaviour. Sufficient statistics can deal with (relative) model indeterminacy and be recovered through reduced-from causal estimations. In both cases, estimated parameters can be plugged into theoretical models in order to derive welfare analysis.

4.3.1 Structural Estimation Fosters Extrapolation

A structural model specifies all the parameters driving the choices of an individual in their optimisation programme. On the one hand, structural behavioural models are very demanding. The functional forms for preferences and biases should be specified and empirical sources should provide enough identifying variability in order to enable the estimation of each parameter.[24] The

---

[24] See DellaVigna (2018) for a thorough presentation of structural behavioural economics.

inability to estimate an incidental parameter may prevent the analyst from recovering key parameters of interest. For instance, lack of information about the effort cost function prevents Rees-Jones (2017) from measuring loss aversion around a zero balance due on tax day. On the other hand, structural behavioural models can be rewarding since they provide a theoretical counterpart to the separation between behavioural biases and preferences in the identification process. Hypotheses about individual decision environments structure the estimation since they constrain the set of subsequent potential actions.

In some situations, the theoretical model is unable to rationalise empirical observations, and hence calls for a new framework. Rabin (2000)'s calibration theorem is one of the most famous examples in BE. According to the expected utility theory, risk aversion comes exclusively from the concavity of the utility function. However, in this framework, Rabin (2000, p. 1282) shows that the choice to turn down small-stakes gambles can only be consistent with an incredibly high level of risk aversion[25] since it would require the marginal utility to decrease at a very fast rate with wealth. He concludes that 'aversion to modest-stakes risk has nothing to do with the diminishing marginal utility of wealth'.

In the case of default options or dominated plans, such calibration results are extreme cases wherein the models' predictions are inconsistent with common empirical observations. In general, inconsistencies may be harder to detect and would call for an assessment of the structurally estimated model through confrontation with external material and alternative theories.

Taking Advantage of Our Model: Internal Validation

Structural models are partly given by the first-order conditions of individual maximisation programmes, which often makes them non-linear and quite complex. Development of original procedures derived from maximum likelihood, minimum distance or methods-of-moments estimations are often needed both to recover the parameters of interest and to deal with the inherent noise in the data. Therefore, standardised test procedures are not always available to assess the internal validity of the estimation.

A model will convincingly capture the behaviour of interest in the data if it is able to replicate some core moments. A graphical presentation of the raw moments and their simulated counterparts can sometimes be a convincing way to ensure that identification sets a close link between theoretical parameters

---

[25] Rabin (2000, p. 1282) gives the following example: 'Suppose that, from any initial wealth level, a person turns down gambles where she loses $100 or gains $110, each with 50 percent probability. Then she will turn down 50–50 bets of losing $1,000 or gaining any sum of money.'

and empirical moments. DellaVigna (2018) even advises re-estimating the model on simulated data to check that estimated parameters do capture and are able to replicate the identifying variability in the data.

Finally, since structural models rely on the simultaneous estimation of a set of parameters, estimated values may be co-dependent. Sensitivity analysis, such as varying exogenously the level of one parameter along a grid and discussing changes in the value of the others, helps in abstracting from this co-dependence. Moreover, it may happen that some values for the parameter of interest are never consistent with empirical observations under any circumstances; then, robustness tests on incidental parameters may efficiently restrict behavioural deviations to a range of credible values.

Taking Advantage of Our Model: Validation in Prediction

The upside of a structural model is that it allows us to estimate policy-invariant parameters. A structural parameter properly estimated in a relevant framework should be used to make accurate forecasts of behavioural responses to policy changes. Therefore, the external validity of a structural model can be assessed on out-of-sample predictions.

Relying on a sample of 22,000 low-income tax filers, Martinez et al. (2022) found evidence of a present bias, especially as the deadline to fill out tax forms approaches. Looking at filing responses around a fiscal reform perceived as altering filing incentives (the 2008 Economic Stimulus Act), they validate in prediction the choice of a quasi-hyperbolic rather than a more standard exponential discounting model. Lardeux (2021) shows that an income tax misperception model estimated in 2011 can be used to predict behavioural responses observed at an irrelevant TT in 2012 following a multiplication by 2.5 of the associated perceived marginal tax rate. A standard model cannot replicate these dynamic adjustments.

Beyond a validation of the underlying set of hypotheses, out-of-sample predictions from structural models are essential to conduct welfare analysis and derive policy recommendations for huge reforms that drive the economy beyond the domain of currently observed policies. This is a major advantage of structural parameters over sufficient statistics, which are always endogenous to current policies and could not be used to extrapolate the consequences of optimal policies (Kleven, 2021).

Taking Advantage of the Literature in Behavioural Economics: External Validity

The strong link between theory and estimation in structural methods is particularly convenient to test assumptions about individual behaviours. Showing that a specific model of behaviour accurately predicts observed choices is not enough. Complementary analysis should provide evidence that concurrent behavioural models have a lower ability to account for them, would imply other behaviours that the data show no trace of or would require implausible parameter values.

In line with this last point, estimations of behavioural models generally benefit from meta-analysis (DellaVigna, 2009). Parametric representations of behavioural theories are often based on standard economic models, wherein behavioural deviations are captured by a single parameter, such as present-bias β in hyperbolic preferences (Laibson, 1997) or loss aversion λ in reference-dependent preferences (Köszegi and Rabin, 2006). A guide for the order of magnitude one should expect is given by the range of previous estimates available in BE.

In a survey of the literature on attention, Gabaix (2019) argues that limited attention can be represented by a single parameter that captures the shrinkage of an opaque attribute in the perceived budget constraint of the behavioural agent. Collecting estimates from several experiments in BE, he shows evidence of an increasing relationship between the level of attention and the relative value of the opaque attribute: the higher the share of this opaque attribute in the budget, the more attention it receives.

Application: DellaVigna, Lindner, Reizer and Schmieder (2017)

Hazard rates out of unemployment are high upon job loss, decrease over time and peak at benefits exhaustion. The standard job search models presented in Mortensen (1986) have a hard time rationalising this pattern, as these models predict an increasing hazard rate out of unemployment until benefits exhaustion and constant afterwards, as depicted by Panel (b) in Figure 7. In order to replicate this empirical fact, such standard models have to assume heterogeneous productivities.

As an alternative behavioural explanation, DellaVigna et al. (2017) assume that unemployed workers are loss-averse and take their recent earnings as an adaptive reference point. Panel (c) in Figure 7 displays the time path of the hazard rate in this case. Job search is high upon job loss since workers incur a painful earnings loss equal to the discrepancy between their previous wage and their UI benefits. Over time, this reference point shifts downward as unemployed workers get used to their status and reduce their search effort. As they get closer to benefits exhaustion, they expect the loss of UI benefits and search harder. Finally, the hazard rate diminishes again if the worker does not find a job before this deadline.

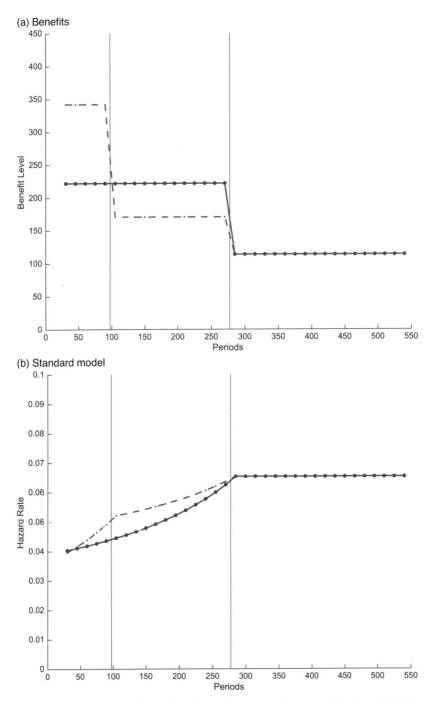

Figure 7 UI benefits and predicted hazard rate as a function of the length of the unemployment spell

In order to determine which one of these two frameworks (standard model with heterogeneous productivities vs. adaptative reference dependence) fits the data best, the authors exploited a reform of the Hungarian unemployment insurance system that created a step in the UI system. They focused on UI claimants who were eligible for the maximum potential duration. Before the implementation of this reform in November 2005, UI benefits were constant, with a replacement rate of 65 percent during the first 270 days of the unemployment spell, after which unemployment assistance would start. This reform introduced a two-step system: claimants get higher benefits during the first

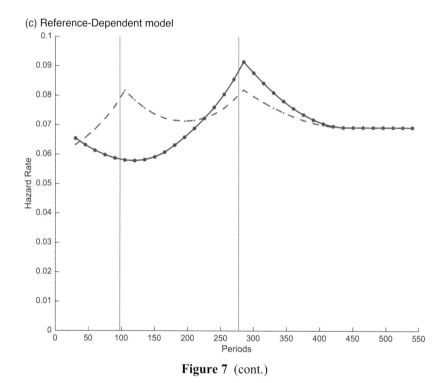

(c) Reference-Dependent model

Figure 7 (cont.)

Caption for Figure 7 (cont.)

Note: Panel (a) shows two benefit regimes, both having a step-down benefit system. After the first step, benefits are higher in the regime represented by the circled blue line than in the regime represented by the red dashed line. After the second step, benefits drop to the same level. Panel (b) shows the hazard rates predicted by the standard model while Panel (c) shows the prediction of the reference-dependent model.

Source: Dellavigna, S., Lindner, A., Reizer, B. and Schmieder, J. F. (2017). Reference-dependent job search: Evidence from Hungary. *The Quarterly Journal of Economics*, 132(4): 1969–2018. [Copyright Oxford University Press; reproduced with permission of *The Quarterly Journal of Economics*].

90 days of their spell and lower benefits afterwards, as displayed by Panel (a) in Figure 7. They conclude that both models perform well to replicate the start of the spell, but reference-dependent preferences outperform the standard model with heterogeneous productivity when it comes to the pattern of the hazard rate around benefit exhaustion.

One of the nicest features of this paper is that even though the authors compare structural models, the estimation of behavioural parameters relies on a natural experiment, which gives great credibility to the identification of individual behavioural adjustments. The elasticity of search effort is identified by the responsiveness of the hazard rate to changes in benefits and the loss aversion parameter λ by the relative magnitude of hazard rates in the pre- versus post-reform period around benefit exhaustion.

The internal validity of their reference-dependent model is evaluated through its ability to replicate empirical hazard rates before and after the reform. Predictions are qualitatively in line with the evolution of hazard rates around the threshold introduced by the reform. The authors are able to relate higher hazard rates both before and after benefits exhaustion to higher expected – and then realised – consumption losses. They further demonstrate that standard job search models cannot account for observed hazard rates. A standard model with heterogeneous optimising agents predicts identical hazard rate upon benefits exhaustion before and after the reform, which is not the case empirically. Assuming time-varying search costs, a delay before the job starts, heterogeneity in re-employment wages or in search elasticities does not provide a better fit of the data.

External validity is assessed using two out-of-sample predictions: the first on another UI reform that raised the duration of unemployment assistance (Panel (a) in Figure 8), the second on another sample of workers with a different UI benefit structure (Panel (b) in Figure 8). The authors compare the reference-dependent model with two versions of the standard model featuring different types of heterogeneity in search costs. Both tests lead to the conclusion that a model with an adaptive reference point displays a better goodness-of-fit compared to alternative standard models.

Finally, empirical investigations further help to refine the model. The authors conclude that exponential discounting is not consistent with the data and reject fixed as well as forward-looking reference points.

4.3.2 Reduced-Form Estimation of Sufficient Statistics

The structural approach is useful to identify specific biases and conduct out-of-sample predictions. However, when the number of equations to estimate is too

(a) Out-of-sample predictions two years prior to reform

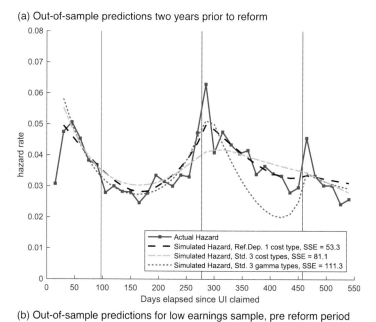

(b) Out-of-sample predictions for low earnings sample, pre reform period

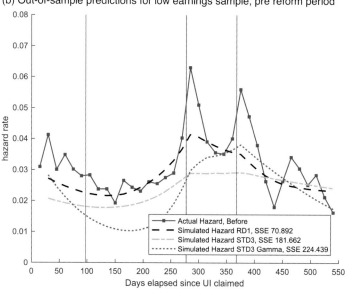

Figure 8 Empirical hazard rates and out-of-sample predictions

Note: The figure shows actual hazard rate out of unemployment, as well as the out-of-sample fit of the reference-dependent model and of two versions of the standard model. Panel (a) shows these hazard rates for the period 2 to 1 years before the reform when unemployment assistance could be claimed until 460 days. Panel (b) shows these hazard rates for individuals who had lower pre-unemployment earnings and thus faced a different benefit path.

Source: Dellavigna, S., Lindner, A., Reizer, B. and Schmieder, J. F. (2017). Reference-dependent job search: Evidence from Hungary. *The Quarterly Journal of Economics*, 132(4): 1969–2018. [Copyright Oxford University Press; reproduced with permission of *The Quarterly Journal of Economics*].

high or when the representation of the bias can be kept general, then a sufficient statistics approach may be privileged.

As discussed in Section 3, for a given economic environment and identical preferences, behavioural deviations generate a discrepancy between the choices of a standard and a behavioural agent or between the choices of the same agent under different frames. As a consequence, biases have first-order welfare effects and alter behavioural responses to fiscal instruments. This incidence should be empirically quantified for policy evaluation.

Sufficient Statistics

As expressed in Equation (5) of Section 3.2.2, the welfare impact of a small variation in the sales tax analysed by Chetty et al. (2009) depends on the identification of the partial demand response $\partial x_b / \partial \tau$ and of the attention parameter θ. The demand response is identified as the observed causal response from the behavioural agent to a variation in the tax rate $d\tau$.

Identification of attention θ is more subtle. Equation (3) implies that a behavioural agent faced with a tax rate τ makes the same choice as a standard agent faced with the tax rate τ_b perceived by the behavioural agent, so $x_b(p, \tau) \equiv x(p, \tau_b)$. In traditional PF, prices and taxes enter the same way in the demand function, which implies that $\partial x / \partial p = \partial x / \partial \tau$. What is really important here is the normative assumption, according to which the behavioural agent is only biased with respect to sales taxes and not with respect to prices: $\partial x_b / \partial p = \partial x / \partial p$. Assuming homogeneous and linear attention such that $\tau_b = \theta \tau$, we have $\partial x_b / \partial \tau = \theta \partial x / \partial \tau$. From these equations, we find the following formula for the parameter of attention:

$$\theta = \frac{\partial x_b / \partial \tau}{\partial x_b / \partial p}.$$

Attention is measured as the relative magnitude of adjustments with respect to changes in the tax rate compared to adjustments with respect to changes in the price of the good. This expression is extremely clear and intuitive. A behavioural agent who over- or underestimates taxes is respectively more ($\theta > 1$) or less ($\theta < 1$) responsive to taxes than to prices. Empirically, the bias is identified from choices under different frames (variations in price vs. variations in taxes) and the estimation of attention θ relies on the causal impact of variations in sales taxes and in prices on the demand for consumption goods.

Causal Framework

Whether in field experiments or using administrative data, PF relies increasingly on causal inference methods to provide concrete policy advice. This relatively recent approach in the econometric evaluation of public policies relies on the Rubin causal framework in order to isolate, show visual evidence of and estimate behavioural responses to fiscal reforms.

The effect of a treatment on an outcome can be inferred through a comparison of the potential outcomes with and without treatment. The problem is that we generally cannot observe different potential outcomes for the same person. A solution is to evaluate this causal impact at an aggregate level: if individuals are randomly assigned to a control or a treatment group, then the Average Treatment Effect (ATE) can be estimated as the difference between the mean outcomes of the two groups. If we suspect that the effect of the treatment is heterogeneous, then we could estimate the Conditional Average Treatment Effect (CATE), which is the ATE conditional on some observable characteristics.

It is often not possible to force people in the treatment group to take the treatment or forbid those in the control group to benefit from it. In such a non-compliance framework, the experimenter can inform the treatment group about the treatment (Imbens, 2014). Some people in the control group will take it anyway while some in the treatment group won't, and the researcher can only recover an Intent-To-Treat (ITT) effect from the difference between the mean outcomes of the two groups. The sample can be divided into four profiles: those who always take the treatment (*always takers*), those who never take it (*never takers*), those who only take it if they are assigned to the treatment (*compliers*) and those who only take it when they are not assigned to the treatment (*defiers*). The type of a given individual remains unknown since they are only observed either in the treatment group or in the control group. Under some assumptions (such as no defiers), this framework enables the estimation of an ATE among compliers or Local Average Treatment Effect (LATE) as the ratio of the ITT over the share of compliers (Imbens, 2010).

This causal framework is particularly convenient in PF where reforms are intended to provide incentives depending on households' characteristics or location. Since they generally aim at inducing specific behaviours according to standard economic models, behavioural biases can be inferred, under specific conditions, from significant empirical deviations from these theoretical predictions. The possibility to rely on informational interventions as a source of exogenous variations is important in PF since treatments often cannot be imposed on citizens. Sometimes, the first step may be of particular interest to the researcher, as in Bhargava and Manoli (2015), who mostly focused on the impact of mailings on the take-up of EITC benefits instead of using the identifying variability introduced by this mailing to estimate the effect of EITC on labour market outcomes.

Two of the most popular methods in applied microeconometrics prove particularly useful to shed light on behavioural deviations: difference-in-differences and the regression discontinuity design.[26]

Difference-in-differences

The difference-in-differences estimation is popular because it is highly efficient for causal inference and quite simple to implement. It can be conducted at the group level. For instance, in order to estimate the impact on demand of posting tax-inclusive price tags, Chetty et al. (2009) consider two control groups in their experiment (see Section 3.1.3): similar products in the same aisle of the treatment store and the same products in other stores. They even conduct a 'triple difference', accounting for differences between treatment and control products and between treatment and control stores over time. Observing each subject individually before and after the treatment enables the estimation of a CATE, as in the experimental framework of Allcott and Taubinsky (2015) described at the end of this section.

Innovative estimation methods have been developed from this framework. Event studies and two-way fixed effects models enable the evaluation of medium- and long-term treatment effects, while synthetic control methods have improved the constitution of control groups.

Regression Discontinuity Design

Bunching estimation exploits individual responses to a local change in incentives around a threshold. The bigger the local bunching mass, the stronger the magnitude of the adjustment. To the contrary, the regression discontinuity design (RDD) relies on the assumption that agents cannot manipulate their characteristics in order to benefit from or avoid a treatment.

Depending on whether they fall on one side of a threshold or the other along an assignment variable, they are assigned a treatment or not. Comparison of outcomes near the threshold identifies treatment effects. Consider the evaluation of extended unemployment benefits on different labour market outcomes, such as unemployment duration (Lalive, 2008; Schmieder et al., 2012a,b, 2016). A causal RDD can be provided by a reform that raises the maximum benefits duration (*treatment*) for some specific claimants, for instance above

---

[26] For a thorough presentation of these econometric methods, see: Wooldridge (2002); Imbens and Lemieux (2008); Angrist and Pischke (2009); Imbens and Wooldridge (2009); Imbens and Rubin (2015); Abadie and Cattaneo (2018); Cattaneo et al. (2020).

a given age (*assignment variable*) threshold. Age is arguably not manipulable, and only old enough claimants face this incentive to stay unemployed longer. Moreover, claimants just below the age threshold are very similar to those just above. Hence, the former can be considered as a control group and the latter as a treatment group that would behave the same way as the control group absent any reform (conditional on observable characteristics). Finally, the average treatment effect on the treated (ATT) can be estimated through a local regression of unemployment duration on extended benefits among claimants close to the age threshold.

One of the most appealing feature of the RDD is its ability to provide visual evidence of behavioural responses to changes in incentives. A sharp variation at the discontinuity in the plot of the outcome on the assignment variable immediately displays these behavioural responses and help convince about their identification. Plotting the density of the assignment variable provides insights regarding its manipulability: absence of bunching indicates that agents are not (locally) optimising with respect to the treatment.

The RDD is adequate to reveal and estimate behavioural deviations from changes in frames. For instance, Feldman et al. (2016) use a discontinuity in the reception of the CTC depending on the child's birthday in order to evaluate the impact of a lump-sum tax change on parental labour supply. The RDD framework has been extended to cases with a sharp change in the treatment probability around the threshold (*fuzzy design*) or in the slope of the treatment function (*regression kink design*[27]).

4.3.3 Application: Allcott and Taubinsky (2015)

In consideration of the optimal subsidy for energy-efficient lightbulbs, Allcott and Taubinsky (2015) provide a clear example of the sufficient statistics methodology. On the one hand, consumers may be subject to an *internality*, in which case they misperceive the relative benefits from energy-efficient CFLs compared to incandescent lightbulbs due to imperfect information or inattention to energy costs. On the other hand, the low demand for CFLs could be related to a stronger preference for incandescent lightbulbs. The design of their experiment disentangles informed preferences from misoptimisation factors.[28]

---

[27] As explained by Card et al. (2015b), in the RKD, the regressor of interest is a kinked function of the assignment variable. For instance, Card et al. (2015a) and Landais (2015) exploit kinks in unemployment benefits schedules, and Nielsen et al. (2010) a kink in the student aid schedule.

[28] The authors do not separate lack of information from behavioural deviations.

Considering the sales taxation framework given by Equation (4), they show that when consumers have heterogeneous relative valuations for CFLs, the optimal subsidy requires two sufficient statistics: the market demand curve $dx_b(p)/d\tau$ and the average marginal bias $b(p)$ estimated at each point on that demand curve. This sufficient statistics approach has at least two very nice features. First, they do not need to specify the type of bias in order to derive welfare analysis, which largely simplifies empirical investigations. Second, bias analysis is not based on a homogeneity assumption.

Once this model is set, they provide an informational treatment about CFLs in order to debias a treatment group. This treatment consists in a comparison of electricity and replacement costs for CFLs and incandescents. The authors are concerned about the risk of inducing experimenter demand effects: treated subjects may want to comply with or defy the treatment. In order to discard such an explanation, they show that their estimates are robust when the treatment also insists on preference-related drawbacks of CFLs: disposal and warm-up time.

They rely on a within-subject design in order to consider heterogeneous biases and potential correlations between the bias and the demand elasticity with respect to the subsidy. This experiment takes place on an online platform called Time-Sharing Experiments for the Social Sciences (TESS). Faced with a multiple price list format, consumers have to choose between CFLs and incandescent lightbulbs for different vectors of prices, both before and after the implementation of the treatment. Hence, the authors are able to estimate the effect of the treatment at each point of the demand curve. Figure 9 displays the demand curves of the treatment and control groups: that is, for each level of relative price, the share of participants who prefer CFLs over incandescent lightbulbs. Compared to the control group, the demand of the treatment group is shifted to the right. When both lightbulbs have the same price, the market share of CFLs is twelve points higher in the treatment group.

Under the assumption that treated subjects are fully debiased, Allcott and Taubinsky (2015) identify the average marginal misoptimisation bias conditional on price as the expected difference between the perceived (relative) value of a CFL before and after the treatment at each level of relative price.

Figure 10 illustrates the welfare analysis behind the determination of the optimal subsidy. The dashed line is the baseline demand curve of the control group. Starting from the market price (relative price equal to 0), a $1 subsidy on CFLs induces a distortion which reduces the market share of incandescent lightbulbs by 12.6 points and generates a welfare loss equal to the red

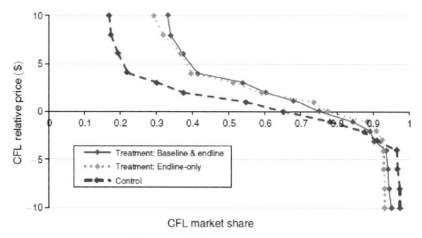

Figure 9 CFLs demand curves

Note: For each level of relative price, this figure shows the share of consumers who choose CFLs over incandescent lightbulbs. Observations are weighted for national representativeness.

Source: Allcott, H. and Taubinsky, D. (2015). Evaluating behaviorally motivated policy: Experimental evidence from the lightbulb market. *American Economic Review*, 105(8): 2501–38. [Copyright American Economic Association; reproduced with permission of the *American Economic Review*].

area below the x-axis and between the first two vertical lines. Just above, the area of the first shaded rectangle on the left reflects welfare gains associated with the internality reduction from this $1 subsidy. The width of this rectangle is equal to the change in market share and its height is equal to the average marginal bias, such that the product of the two captures the value of inducing consumers to buy products that are more valuable to them than they realise.

The same logic applies for the marginal impact of a $2 subsidy and so on. The optimal $3 subsidy on CFLs is the maximum amount such that the marginal welfare gain from internality reduction exceeds the marginal welfare loss from distortions.

5 Conclusion: Policies Targeting Behavioural Agents

Previous sections went through the introduction of behavioural agents in PF, discussed the identification of behavioural deviations and presented a wide range of estimation procedures and sources of information.

This final section wraps up this Element with a discussion of the implications for fiscal policy design. Behavioural deviations fundamentally challenge the

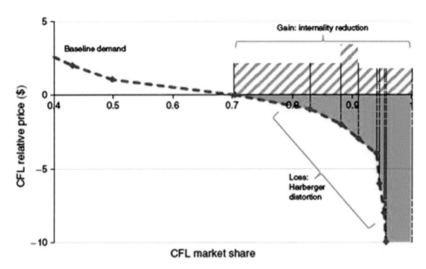

Figure 10 Welfare analysis and optimal subsidy
Note: This figure illustrates the welfare effects of increases in the CFL subsidy using the
TESS experiment results. Observations are weighted for national representativeness.
Source: Allcott, H. and Taubinsky, D. (2015). Evaluating behaviorally motivated policy:
Experimental evidence from the lightbulb market. *American Economic Review*, 105(8):
2501–38. [Copyright American Economic Association; reproduced with permission of
the *American Economic Review*].

notion of welfare on which optimal fiscal policies are based. Efficient and
equitable real-life policies should take bias heterogeneity into account, especially when these deviations maintain households in poverty traps.
Governments can rely on 'nudges' as new fiscal instruments in order to
implement these objectives.

5.1 Which Policy Should the Social Planner Promote?

In the preceding sections, the design of policies for behavioural agents relies
on two strong assumptions, which are discussed from a welfare perspective
here. First, the social planner is able to label some behaviours as *biased*,
which implies a normative reference. Second, an optimal policy should bring
individual decisions closer to the choices of a standard unbiased economic
agent.

5.1.1 Normal or Biased Behaviour?

Biased behaviours can be characterised as psychological deviations from some
normal (unbiased) reference wherein choices reveal preferences. In a welfare
perspective, preferences differ from frames in that only preferences are relevant

to assess the welfare of an individual. Frames can change the way agents take decisions, but they do not alter individual welfare. Bernheim and Rangel (2009) and Bernheim and Taubinsky (2018) propose the concept of a *welfare-relevant domain* of choices that directly inform the observer about individual preferences, such that preferences can be recovered through standard inference.

They define this domain by the exclusion of choices that express incorrectly informed judgements or *mistakes*. These choices are characterised by two features: choice reversal and characterisation failure.[29] Choice reversal challenges the WARP, since agents change their choices between two available bundles, for instance due to framing effects. Characterisation failure occurs when agents do not make the connection between the available options and their consequences, even though they have perfect access to complete and relevant information. This second condition grounds the need, discussed in Section 4.1.3, to make a distinction between uninformed choices and behavioural biases.

Under these conditions, some behaviours can be identified as biased. For instance, choice reversals happen when Chetty et al. (2009) display tax-inclusive price tags, since consumers buy less of these products. Characterisation failure lies in the fact that although consumers are able to provide the value of the sales tax rate in a survey, they do not take it fully into account when shopping. In this case, the welfare-relevant domain is characterised by the choice of a consumer for whom sales taxes are fully salient.

5.1.2 Optimal Policy for Behavioural Agents

Beyond identification of biased behaviours, the social planner should take a normative stand on bias correction. Optimal policies correcting for behavioural biases should be based on welfare-relevant preferences. When individual choices reflect a misperception or a misoptimisation issue, there is often a way to reframe the decision environment, such that subjects behave as a standard economic agent and reveal their preferences. It is much more complex when it comes to recovering their experienced utility.

In Section 3, we assumed that the social planner knows both the decision utility v and the experienced utility u, and determines the optimal policy according to the latter taking into account behavioural responses according to the former. However, in practice, there is no obvious way to recover the experienced utility, since, as explained in Section 4, textbook inference is based on preferences revealed by observed decisions. Going from positive to

---

[29] Hence, this domain does not exclude inconsistencies. See Bernheim and Taubinsky (2018) for a discussion of restrictions to a domain of consistent choices.

normative conclusions requires further assumptions in order to circumvent welfare-relevant preferences.

In order to quantify precisely the experienced utility, Kahneman (2000) suggests measuring *moment-based happiness* at multiple points in time over the course of this experience. Taking the case of smokers, Gruber and Mullainathan (2005) illustrate why the decision utility is not sufficient in order to evaluate the welfare impact of cigarette taxes. According to the standard theory, smokers reduce their consumption of cigarettes when taxes are increased. However, this behaviour is consistent with two different models that have very different welfare conclusions. On the one hand, a 'rational addiction' model predicts a welfare loss since cigarettes get more expensive. On the other hand, time-inconsistent smokers may find it difficult to quit smoking if they have a tendency to over-estimate their propensity to quit smoking in the future and have no way to tie their hands in the present. In this case, cigarette taxes would act as a self-control device and ultimately increase their welfare. In order to discriminate between these two models, Gruber and Mullainathan (2005) measure the impact of cigarette excise taxation on self-reported happiness and find that higher taxes make smokers happier. Such empirical evidence is consistent with a model of sophisticated present-biased consumers, and cigarette taxes can be considered as a commitment device from a welfare perspective.

A recent approach relies on the choice of experts as a normative reference. In an attempt to determine the optimal tax policy to address the consumption of sugary drinks without increasing earnings inequalities, Allcott et al. (2019) collected information about the purchases of 20,000 consumers and constructed survey measures of their nutrition knowledge and self-control. They showed that nutritionists score high on this test and shed light on strong negative correlations between these measures and soda consumption. Then, the authors predicted a normative level of soda consumption for each household, assuming that they have the nutrition knowledge of a dietitian and no self-control issue. The welfare-relevant domain is directly characterised using a survey, and any deviation from this domain is quantified using observed consumption choices. As stressed by the authors, this 'rational consumer benchmark' relies on the identifying assumption that unobserved preferences are conditionally uncorrelated with the internality bias. From a policy design perspective, the social planner wants to bring consumers' choices closer to the consumption of a dietician, which is a fairly strong position if this expert has singular preferences stemming from a personal conception of a healthy body or healthy diets.

Finally, welfare-relevant preferences are hardly identifiable when individual choices are observed under only one frame. Madrian and Shea (2001) considered choices of enrolment in 401(k) retirement saving plans among 10,000 employees at a US firm. As in most companies, employees had to actively opt into this plan, but the firm changed this frame such that afterwards employees were automatically enrolled at a 3 per cent contribution rate and could opt out. The key finding of this paper holds in a simple statistic: before this change of frame was implemented, less than half of employees used to participate in this plan, whereas they were 86 per cent under automatic enrolment, even though the main features of this retirement plan remained unchanged over time. Moreover, information about 401(k) plans was easily accessible and transaction costs associated with enrolment remained small. Which default option should the government promote: opt-in or opt-out? Faced with such *normative ambiguity*, the planner does not know which frame is relevant for welfare. Thaler and Sunstein (2003) argue that revealed choices can partly inform optimal default. Since many employees end up opting-in under the no-enrolment default, whereas few of them opt-out under automatic enrolment, the latter policy would appear preferable. In order to resolve this normative ambiguity, Goldin and Reck (2022) proposed an estimator for the cognitive cost associated with the selection of a non-default option. They expressed optimal defaults as a function of the share of this cost that enters the experienced utility of the decision-maker. When this share is low, the optimal policy is to induce agents to make active decisions (suppression of the default option). When this share is high, it is optimal to set a default such that few people opt out.

5.2 Heterogeneous Behavioural Deviations

Behavioural agents may display different combinations of biases with different intensities, may be more or less aware of their bias and may adapt to variations in their economic environment. Behavioural heterogeneity strongly determines policy recommendations.

5.2.1 Combinations

In order to simplify the presentation of this Element, most examples featured only one specific behavioural bias. However, empirical evidence may sometimes only be explained by a combination of biases. For instance, in the investigation discussed in Section 4.3.1, DellaVigna et al. (2017) conclude that the model that best fits the pattern of hazard rates along the unemployment spell features recent income as a reference point and substantial impatience. Welfare analyses that do not require a precise estimation of the type of bias provide another way to deal with a potential multiplicity of biases.

Assuming homogeneously biased agents, Chetty et al. (2009) estimate a low dead-weight loss from sales taxes since partially attentive agents are not responsive to the tax rate. However, in their lab-in-the-field experiment summarised in Section 4.2.1, Taubinsky and Rees-Jones (2018) observe substantial bias heterogeneity. Adapting the behavioural sales tax model in order to account for different degrees of consumer attention, they show that Equation (5) of Section 3.2.2 becomes:

$$\frac{dW}{d\tau} \approx \tau E[\theta|p,\tau]\frac{dx_b}{d\tau} + \tau Var[\theta \,|\, p,\tau]\frac{dx_b}{dp},$$

where $E[\theta|p,\tau]$ and $V[\theta|p,\tau]$ are, respectively, the mean and variance of attention θ among consumers indifferent about buying the good at price $p + \tau$. Limited attention supports tax increases since agents are less responsive. However, heterogeneous inattention dampens this effect as a result of a mismatch between consumers and products: some agents willing to pay for the good will not buy it because they overestimate sales taxes, while inattentive agents will buy it despite a low willingness to pay. This mismatch increases the deadweight loss from taxation, hence calling for a lower optimal tax rate compared to homogeneous attention.

Beyond the pure degree of bias heterogeneity, the redistributive consequences of fiscal policies require an investigation of the correlations between biases and financial characteristics. According to Bertrand et al. (2004), Mullainathan and Shafir (2013) and Schilbach et al. (2016), humans act on a mental bandwidth, which captures mental availability and capacities. The mental bandwidth of a poor house-hold is strongly impaired by their living conditions (such as sleep deprivation), their inability to externalise household production (e.g. hiring a housekeeper) and the necessity to juggle time- and brain-consuming tasks related to their condition, such as frequently asking for welfare benefits or going to job interviews. Consequently, behavioural biases may be much more detrimental for these populations and may lock them in poverty traps (Banerjee and Mullainathan, 2008). Focused on present emergencies, they may procrastinate on filling out administrative forms in order to receive benefits or take credit cards with high borrowing interest rates and hidden costs. Randomly assigning a cognitive survey to low-income households, Carvalho et al. (2016) found that subjects appeared more present-biased with respect to monetary outcomes before payday, consistent with liquidity constraints.

Not all behavioural agents passively endure the consequences of their biases. A distinction between *naive* and *sophisticated* agents has been developed by the literature on hyperbolic preferences (Laibson, 1997; O'Donoghue and Rabin, 1999) to separate behavioural agents depending on whether or not they are conscious of their biases. Naive agents never take into account their present bias, which gives rise to procrastination behaviours whereby each period they report painful tasks to the next period and remain convinced that they will achieve them. In contrast, sophisticated agents are aware of their biases and try to develop control over them, for instance through commitment devices (Schilbach, 2019).

Behavioural agents may further endogenously adapt their biases according to the economic circumstances. In his review of behavioural inattention, Gabaix (2019) cites a literature on rational attention based on the assumption that in a complex environment, agents allocate attention to the most salient and economically relevant features for their maximisation programme. They cannot attend to all dimensions of the economy, but actively target the most important and easily accessible ones. As discussed in Section 4.2.1, Taubinsky and Rees-Jones (2018) find evidence in favour of endogenous attention, which increases with the size of sales taxes.

5.3 Standard or Behavioural Instruments?

This Element is mostly about the design of standard fiscal instruments. However, behavioural interventions are increasingly used in order to guide agents towards presumably welfare-enhancing policies. If the literature on *nudges* is too large to be summarised here,[30] we may learn a few lessons from the specific treatment of nudges in PF. More generally, PF can rely on *choice architecture* in order to determine the optimal structure for the public sector.

5.3.1 Nudges as Fiscal Instruments

Thaler and Sunstein (2003) and Sunstein and Thaler (2009) define *nudges* as libertarian paternalistic policies: paternalistic because the government changes the way fiscal policies are framed (*choice architecture*) in order to influence presumably biased people towards presumably good behaviours, but also libertarian since nudges do not constrain individual choice sets. Formally, in contrast with traditional fiscal instruments such as taxes and transfers, nudges change the programme people are maximising without altering their budget set.[31] The

---

[30] For several examples of nudges as public policies, see OECD (2017) and Gabuthy et al. (2021).

[31] There is no strict consensus on the definition of nudges in PF. Bernheim and Taubinsky (2018, p. 442) consider a more restrictive definition: 'We define a nudge more precisely as a non-price intervention that achieves a change in behavior by modifying the decision problem in a way that would not alter a consumer's perception of the opportunity set absent some error in reasoning.'

preceding sections have already presented a common type of nudge: informal interventions (Bhargava and Manoli, 2015; Finkelstein and Notowidigdo, 2019; Boutchenik and Lardeux, 2020).

Nudges have costs (sending letters, calling people on the phone, setting up meetings or individual welfare costs of being reminded of a social norm) and arguably generate some benefits for society in the form of fiscal revenue and welfare gains. Hence, they should be evaluated through a welfare analysis as any other fiscal instrument. For instance, Allcott and Kessler (2019) estimate a strong impact of the Home Energy Reports policy: a letter comparing households' energy consumption to that of their neighbours triggers large behavioural responses at low costs. However, a simple cost–benefit analysis overstates the welfare gains from this policy by $620 million because it ignores the social pressure exerted by reports on recipients. These negative consequences can be more obvious when they imply lower revenues. Damgaard and Gravert (2018) warn charitable organisations against strong reminders. If they can efficiently nudge some contributors into sending more money, others may perceive this pressure as too invasive and unsubscribe from the mailing list. In this case, negative welfare consequences directly translate into an outflow of donations. Finally, as stressed by Handel (2013), nudges can be particularly harmful when they exacerbate adverse selection issues.

5.3.2 A Behavioural View of the Public Sector

Beyond the use of some nudges as instruments, lessons from BE question the structure of the whole public sector. Is it always better to design simple tax systems? Should social benefits be claimed by potential recipients or automated?

According to Kleven and Kopczuk (2011), a complex design for welfare benefits systems can be used as a screening device in order to target the neediest households, under the assumption that this population will engage in claiming benefits because their potential gains exceed search and information costs. This perspective on optimal transfers is in line with the literature on *ordeal mechanisms* (Nichols and Zeckhauser, 1982), according to which tedious administrative procedures may deter agents with a low marginal utility from claiming welfare benefits. Beyond this pure deadweight cost effect, Kleven and Kopczuk (2011) argue that complex tasks such as proving compliance with eligibility criteria or providing the correct supporting documents are also useful in order to screen between deserving and undeserving applicants and thereby improve targeting efficiency.

Hence, they exclude from this definition interventions that directly alter individual welfare (e.g. graphic imagery on cigarette packs or reduction in cognitive costs).

In contrast, empirical investigations indicate that the poorest individuals are also less prone to understand complex systems (Dynarski and Scott–Clayton, 2006; Mullainathan and Shafir, 2013). Providing information and assistance to elderly Americans potentially eligible for the SNAP programme (see Section 4.2.1 for a description of this field experiment), Finkelstein and Notowidigdo (2019) observe a tendency to underestimate expected benefits, which is particularly strong among needier people. However, this empirical fact is not sufficient to support a debiasing intervention. For the purpose of a social welfare analysis, they advise collecting information about the distributions of misperceptions and costs (processing applications, additional benefits paid to new claimants) across individuals. If households misperceive the benefits from applying, then information interventions can generate first-order welfare gains for marginal applicants.[32] Even though their intervention decreases targeting (marginal recipients receive lower benefits and are less sick than average ones), the authors conclude in favour of small welfare gains, which suggests that there would be 'a cost-effective way of redistributing to low-income individuals'.

Automatic enrolment would be a radically opposite solution. Eligible households fail to claim welfare benefits for various reasons, including transactions costs, self-control issues, limited optimisation capacities, social stigma or even, in the case of liquidity constrained households, a fear of having to reimburse undue payments. By placing the burden of eligibility proof on the administration rather than on claimants, automatic enrolment would effectively suppress the incidence of many of these issues on the receipt of social benefits. Making these benefits less salient through automation could reduce the focus on negative incentives related to the loss of welfare benefits when taking a new job. Stigma can prove particularly hard to measure since it involves a meta-choice (Köszegi and Rabin, 2008): eligible individuals not only have preferences over benefits, but also over the choice to claim them. Hence, they could be better off if the social planner decides to allocate them these benefits, which they would never have claimed themselves. Automatic enrolment restricts their choice set, enabling the possibility that someone else acknowledges their claimant status. A welfare evaluation of automatic enrolment should balance the cost associated with additional recipients against the welfare gains from the time saved, the lower cognitive burden and the lower social stigma. These analyses could lead to fruitful developments in the field of BPF.

---

[32] By the same logic as presented in Section 3, since the envelop theorem does not hold for behavioural agents.

References

Aaron, H., ed. (1999). *Behavioural Dimensions of Retirement Economics*. Brookings Institution Press.

Abadie, A. and Cattaneo, M. D. (2018). Econometric methods for program evaluation. *Annual Review of Economics*, 10(1):465–503.

Abeler, J. and Jäger, S. (2015). Complex tax incentives. *American Economic Journal: Economic Policy*, 7(3):1–28.

Allcott, H. and Kessler, J. B. (2019). The welfare effects of nudges: A case study of energy use social comparisons. *American Economic Journal: Applied Economics*, 11(1):236–76.

Allcott, H., Lockwood, B. B. and Taubinsky, D. (2019). Regressive sin taxes, with an application to the optimal soda tax. *Quarterly Journal of Economics*, 134(3):1557–626.

Allcott, H. and Taubinsky, D. (2015). Evaluating behaviorally motivated policy: Experimental evidence from the lightbulb market. *American Economic Review*, 105(8):2501–38.

Andreoni, J., Erard, B. and Feinstein, J. (1998). Tax compliance. *Journal of Economic Literature*, 36(2):818–60.

Angrist, J. and Pischke, J.-S. (2009). *Mostly Harmless Econometrics: An Empiricist's Companion*. Princeton University Press, 1st ed.

Atkinson, A. B. and Stiglitz, J. E. (2015). *Lectures on Public Economics: Updated edition*. Number 10493 in Economics Books. Princeton University Press.

Auerbach, A. and Feldstein, M., eds. (2013). *Handbook of Public Economics*, volumes 1–5. North-Holland.

Babcock, L., Congdon, W., Katz, L. and Mullainathan, S. (2012). Notes on behavioral economics and labor market policy. *IZA Journal of Labor Policy*, 1(1):1–14.

Baicker, K., Mullainathan, S. and Schwartzstein, J. (2015). Behavioral hazard in health insurance. *The Quarterly Journal of Economics*, 130(4):1623–67.

Baily, M. N. (1978). Some aspects of optimal unemployment insurance. *Journal of Public Economics*, 10(3):379–402.

Banerjee, A. V. and Duflo, E., eds. (2017). *Handbook of Field Experiments*. North-Holland.

Banerjee, A. V. and Mullainathan, S. (2008). Limited attention and income distribution. *American Economic Review*, 98(2):489–93.

Bardsley, N., Cubitt, R., Loomes, G. et al. (2010). *Experimental Economics: Rethinking the Rules*. Princeton University Press.

Benjamin, D. J., Heffetz, O., Kimball, M. S. and Rees-Jones, A. (2014). Can marginal rates of substitution be inferred from happiness data? Evidence from residency choices. *American Economic Review*, 104(11):3498–528.

Benzarti, Y. (2017). How taxing is tax filing? Using revealed preferences to estimate compliance costs. *American Economic Journal: Economic* Policy, 12(4):38–57.

Bernheim, B. D. (2009). Behavioral welfare economics. *Journal of the European Economic Association*, 7(2/3):267–319.

Bernheim, B. D. and Rangel, A. (2009). Beyond revealed preference: Choice-theoretic foundations for behavioral welfare economics. *The Quarterly Journal of Economics*, 124(1):51–104.

Bernheim, B. D. and Taubinsky, D. (2018). Behavioral public economics. In Bernheim, B. D., DellaVigna, S. and Laibson, D., eds., *Handbook of Behavioral Economics: Foundations and Applications 1*, volume 1, section 5, pages 381–516. North-Holland.

Bertrand, M. and Mullainathan, S. (2001). Do people mean what they say? Implications for subjective survey data. *American Economic Review*, 91(2):67–72.

Bertrand, M., Mullainathan, S. and Shafir, E. (2004). A behavioral-economics view of poverty. *American Economic Review*, 94(2):419–23.

Beshears, J., Choi, J. J., Laibson, D. and Madrian, B. C. (2018). Behavioral household finance. In Bernheim, B. D., DellaVigna, S. and Laibson, D., eds., *Handbook of Behavioral Economics: Foundations and Applications 1*, volume 1, section 3, pages 177–276. North-Holland.

Bettinger, E. P., Long, B. T., Oreopoulos, P. and Sanbonmatsu, L. (2012). The role of application assistance and information in college decisions: Results from the H&R Block FAFSA experiment. *The Quarterly Journal of Economics*, 127(3):1205–42.

Bhargava, S., Loewenstein, G. and Sydnor, J. (2017). Choose to lose: Health plan choices from a menu with dominated option. *The Quarterly Journal of Economics*, 132(3):1319–72.

Bhargava, S. and Manoli, D. (2015). Psychological frictions and the incomplete take-up of social benefits: Evidence from an IRS field experiment. *American Economic Review*, 105(11):3489–529.

Boutchenik, B. and Lardeux, R. (2020). The take-up of unemployment benefit extensions. INSEE Working Papers G2020-02, Institut National de la Statistique et des Etudes Economiques.

Card, D., Johnston, A., Leung, P., Mas, A. and Pei, Z. (2015a). The effect of unemployment benefits on the duration of unemployment insurance receipt:

New evidence from a regression kink design in Missouri, 2003–2013. *American Economic Review*, 105(5):126–30.

Card, D., Lee, D. S., Pei, Z. and Weber, A. (2015b). Inference on causal effects in a generalized regression kink design. *Econometrica*, 83(6):2453–83.

Carson, R. T. (2012). Contingent valuation: A practical alternative when prices aren't available. *Journal of Economic Perspectives*, 26(4):27–42.

Carvalho, L. S., Meier, S. and Wang, S. W. (2016). Poverty and economic decision-making: Evidence from changes in financial resources at payday. *American Economic Review*, 106(2):260–84.

Cattaneo, M. D., Idrobo, N. and Titiunik, R. (2020). *A Practical Introduction to Regression Discontinuity Designs: Foundations*. Elements in Quantitative and Computational Methods for the Social Sciences. Cambridge University Press.

Chandra, A., Handel, B. and Schwartzstein, J. (2019). Behavioral economics and health-care markets. In Bernheim, B. D., DellaVigna, S. and Laibson, D., eds., *Handbook of Behavioral Economics Foundations and Applications 2*, volume 2, section 6, pages 459–502. North-Holland.

Chang, T. Y., Huang, W. and Wang, Y. (2018). Something in the air: Pollution and the demand for health insurance. *Review of Economic Studies*, 85(3):1609–34.

Chetty, R. (2006). A general formula for the optimal level of social insurance. *Journal of Public Economics*, 90(10):1879–901.

Chetty, R. (2009). Sufficient statistics for welfare analysis: A bridge between structural and reduced-form methods. *Annual Review of Economics*, 1(1):451–88.

Chetty, R. (2015). Behavioral economics and public policy: A pragmatic perspective. *American Economic Review*, 105(5):1–33.

Chetty, R. and Finkelstein, A. (2013). Social insurance: Connecting theory to data. In Auerbach, A., Chetty, R., Feldstein, M. and Saez, E., eds., *Handbook of Public Economics*, volume 5, Section 3, pages 111–93. North-Holland.

Chetty, R., Friedman, J. N. and Saez, E. (2013). Using differences in knowledge across neighborhoods to uncover the impacts of the EITC on earnings. *American Economic Review*, 103(7):2683–721.

Chetty, R., Looney, A. and Kroft, K. (2009). Salience and taxation: Theory and evidence. *American Economic Review*, 99(4):1145–77.

Congdon, W. J., Kling, J. R. and Mullainathan, S. (2011). *Policy and Choice: Public Finance through the Lens of Behavioral Economics*. Brookings Institution Press.

Cruces, G., Perez-Truglia, R. and Tetaz, M. (2013). Biased perceptions of income distribution and preferences for redistribution: Evidence from a survey experiment. *Journal of Public Economics*, 98:100–12.

Currie, J. (2006). *The Take-Up of Social Benefits*. Russell Sage Foundation.

Damgaard, M. T. and Gravert, C. (2018). The hidden costs of nudging: Experimental evidence from reminders in fundraising. *Journal of Public Economics*, 157:15–26.

DellaVigna, S. (2009). Psychology and economics: Evidence from the field. *Journal of Economic Literature*, 47(2):315–72.

DellaVigna, S. (2018). Structural behavioral economics. In Bernheim, B. D., DellaVigna, S. and Laibson, D., eds., *Handbook of Behavioral Economics: Foundations and Applications 1*, volume 1, chapter 7, pages 613–723. North-Holland.

DellaVigna, S., Heining, J., Schmieder, J. F. and Trenkle, S. (2022). Evidence on job search models from a survey of unemployed workers in Germany. *The Quarterly Journal of Economics*, 137(2):1181–1232.

DellaVigna, S., Lindner, A., Reizer, B. and Schmieder, J. F. (2017). Reference-dependent job search: Evidence from Hungary. *The Quarterly Journal of Economics*, 132(4):1969–2018.

Di Tella, R. and MacCulloch, R. (2006). Some uses of happiness data in economics. *Journal of Economic Perspectives*, 20(1):25–46.

Diamond, P. and Vartiainen, H. (2012). *Behavioral Economics and Its Applications*. Princeton University Press.

Dohmen, T. (2014). Behavioral labor economics: Advances and future directions. *Labour Economics*, 30(C):71–85.

Durlauf, S. and Blume, L. (2009). *Behavioural and Experimental Economics*. The New Palgrave Economics Collection. Palgrave Macmillan.

Dynarski, S. M. and Scott–Clayton, J. E. (2006). The cost of complexity in federal student aid: Lessons From optimal tax theory and behavioral economics. *National Tax Journal*, 59(2):319–56.

Farhi, E. and Gabaix, X. (2020). Optimal taxation with behavioral agents. *American Economic Review*, 110(1):298–336.

Fehr, E., Goette, L. and Zehnder, C. (2009). A behavioral account of the labor market: The role of fairness concerns. *Annual Review of Economics*, 1(1):355–84.

Feldman, N. E., Katuščák, P. and Kawano, L. (2016). Taxpayer confusion: Evidence from the child tax credit. *American Economic Review*, 106(3):807–35.

Finkelstein, A. (2009). E-ztax: Tax salience and tax rates. *The Quarterly Journal of Economics*, 124(3):969.

Finkelstein, A. and Notowidigdo, M. J. (2019). Take-up and targeting: Experimental evidence from SNAP. *The Quarterly Journal of Economics*, 134(3):1505–56.

Frank, R. G. (2012). Behavioral economics and health economics. In Diamond, P. and Vartiainen, H., eds., *Behavioral Economics and Its Applications*, pages 195–234. Princeton University Press.

Frey, B. S. and Stutzer, A. (2002). What can economists learn from happiness research? *Journal of Economic Literature*, 40(2):402–35.

Gabaix, X. (2014). A sparsity-based model of bounded rationality. *The Quarterly Journal of Economics*, 129(4):1661.

Gabaix, X. (2019). Behavioral Inattention. In Bernheim, B. D., DellaVigna, S. and Laibson, D., eds., *Handbook of Behavioral Economics: Foundations and Applications 2*, volume 2, chapter 4, pages 261–343. North-Holland.

Gabuthy, Y., Jacquemet, N. and L'Haridon, O. (2021). *Économie comportementale des politiques publiques*. La Découverte.

Ganong, P. and Noel, P. (2019). Consumer spending during unemployment: Positive and normative implications. *American Economic Review*, 109(7):2383–424.

Gerritsen, A. (2016). Optimal taxation when people do not maximize well-being. *Journal of Public Economics*, 144:122–39.

Gneezy, U. and Imas, A. (2017). Lab in the field: Measuring preferences in the wild. In Banerjee, A. V. and Duflo, E., eds., *Handbook of Field Experiments*, volume 1, chapter 10, pages 439–64. North-Holland.

Goldin, J. and Homonoff, T. (2013). Smoke gets in your eyes: Cigarette tax salience and regressivity. *American Economic Journal: Economic Policy*, 5(1):302–36.

Goldin, J. and Reck, D. (2022). Optimal defaults with normative ambiguity. *Review of Economics and* Statistics, 104(1):17–33.

Gruber, J. (2015). *Public Finance and Public Policy*. Macmillan Learning.

Gruber, J. and Köszegi, B. (2004). Tax incidence when individuals are time-inconsistent: The case of cigarette excise taxes. *Journal of Public Economics*, 88(9):1959–87.

Gruber, J. H. and Mullainathan, S. (2005). Do cigarette taxes make smokers happier. *The BE Journal of Economic Analysis & Policy*, 5(1):1–45.

Handel, B. and Schwartzstein, J. (2018). Frictions or mental gaps: What's behind the information we (don't) use and when do we care? *Journal of Economic Perspectives*, 32(1):155–78.

Handel, B. R. (2013). Adverse selection and inertia in health insurance markets: When nudging hurts. *American Economic Review*, 103(7):2643–82.

Handel, B. R. and Kolstad, J. T. (2015). Health insurance for 'humans': Information frictions, plan choice, and consumer welfare. *American Economic Review*, 105(8):2449–500.

Harberger, A. C. (1964). The measurement of waste. *The American Economic Review*, 54(3):58–76.

Hastings, J. and Shapiro, J. M. (2018). How are snap benefits spent? Evidence from a retail panel. *American Economic Review*, 108(12):3493–540.

Hopenhayn, H. A. and Nicolini, J. P. (1997). Optimal unemployment insurance. *Journal of Political Economy*, 105(2):412–38.

Imbens, G. and Lemieux, T. (2008). Regression discontinuity designs: A guide to practice. *Journal of Econometrics*, 142(2):615–35.

Imbens, G. W. (2010). Better late than nothing: Some comments on Deaton (2009) and Heckman and Urzua (2009). *Journal of Economic Literature*, 48(2):399–423.

Imbens, G. W. (2014). Instrumental variables: An econometrician's perspective. *Statistical Science*, 29(3):323–58.

Imbens, G. W. and Rubin, D. B. (2015). *Causal Inference for Statistics, Social, and Biomedical Sciences: An Introduction*. Cambridge University Press.

Imbens, G. W. and Wooldridge, J. M. (2009). Recent developments in the econometrics of program evaluation. *Journal of Economic Literature*, 47(1):5–86.

Ito, K. (2014). Do consumers respond to marginal or average price? Evidence from nonlinear electricity pricing. *American Economic Review*, 104(2):537–63.

Jacquemet, N. and L'Haridon, O. (2018). *Experimental Economics: Method and Applications*. Cambridge University Press.

Jacquemet, N., Luchini, S. and Malézieux, A. (2020). *Comment lutter contre la fraude fiscale? Les enseignements de l'économie comportementale*. CEPREMAP. Éditions Rue d'Ulm.

Kagel, J. H. and Roth, A. E., eds. (1995). *The Handbook of Experimental Economics*. Princeton University Press.

Kahneman, D. (2000). Experienced utility and objective happiness: A moment-based approach, in A. Tversky and D. Kahneman, eds., *Choices, Values and Frames*, pages 673–92. Cambridge: Cambridge University Press.

Kahneman, D. (2011). *Thinking, fast and slow*. Farrar, Straus and Giroux.

Kahneman, D., Diener, E. and Schwarz, N., eds. (1999). *Well-Being: Foundations of Hedonic Psychology*. Russell Sage Foundation.

Kahneman, D. and Sugden, R. (2005). Experienced utility as a standard of policy evaluation. *Environmental and Resource Economics*, 32:161–81.

Kahneman, D., Wakker, P. P. and Sarin, R. (1997). Back to Bentham? Explorations of experienced utility. *The Quarterly Journal of Economics*, 112(2):375–406.

Kirchler, E. and Braithwaite, V. (2007). *The Economic Psychology of Tax Behaviour*. Cambridge University Press.

Kleven, H. (2021). Sufficient statistics revisited. *Annual Review of Economics*, 13:515–38.

Kleven, H. J. (2016). Bunching. *Annual Review of Economics*, 8:435–64.

Kleven, H. J. and Kopczuk, W. (2011). Transfer program complexity and the take-up of social benefits. *American Economic Journal: Economic Policy*, 3(1):54–90.

Kleven, H. J. and Waseem, M. (2013). Using notches to uncover optimization frictions and structural elasticities: Theory and evidence from Pakistan. *The Quarterly Journal of Economics*, 128(2):669–723.

Kopczuk, W. (2005). Tax bases, tax rates and the elasticity of reported income. *Journal of Public Economics*, 89(11):2093–119.

Köszegi, B. and Rabin, M. (2006). A model of reference-dependent preferences. *The Quarterly Journal of Economics*, 121(4):1133–65.

Köszegi, B. and Rabin, M. (2008). Choices, situations, and happiness. *Journal of Public Economics*, 92(8–9):1821–32.

Kroft, K., Kucko, K., Lehmann, E. and Schmieder, J. (2020). Optimal income taxation with unemployment and wage responses: A sufficient statistics approach. *American Economic Journal: Economic Policy*, 12(1): 254–92.

Laibson, D. (1997). Golden eggs and hyperbolic discounting. *The Quarterly Journal of Economics*, 112(2):443–78.

Lalive, R. (2008). How do extended benefits affect unemployment duration? A regression discontinuity approach. *Journal of Econometrics*, 142(2):785–806.

Landais, C. (2015). Assessing the welfare effects of unemployment benefits using the regression kink design. *American Economic Journal: Economic Policy*, 7(4):243–78.

Landais, C., Michaillat, P., and Saez, E. (2018a). A macroeconomic approach to optimal unemployment insurance: Applications. *American Economic Journal: Economic Policy*, 10(2):182–216.

Landais, C., Michaillat, P., and Saez, E. (2018b). A macroeconomic approach to optimal unemployment insurance: Theory. *American Economic Journal: Economic Policy*, 10(2):152–81.

Lardeux, R. (2021). Behavioral cross-influence of a shadow tax bracket: Evidence from bunching where tax liabilities start. CRED Working Paper 5, CRED – Université Paris II.

Lavecchia, A. M., Liu, H. and Oreopoulos, P. (2016). Behavioral economics of education: Progress and possibilities. In Hanushek, E. A., Machin, S. and Woessmann, L., eds., *Handbook of the Economics of Education*, volume 5, chapter 1, pages 1–74. Elsevier.

Ledyard, J. O. (1995). *Public Goods: A Survey of Experimental Research*, chapter 2, pages 111–94. Princeton University Press.

Lehmann, E., Marical, F. and Rioux, L. (2013). Labor income responds differently to income-tax and payroll-tax reforms. *Journal of Public Economics*, 99(C):66–84.

Madrian, B. C. and Shea, D. F. (2001). The power of suggestion: Inertia in 401(k) participation and savings behavior. *The Quarterly Journal of Economics*, 116(4):1149–87.

Manski, C. F. (2004). Measuring expectations. *Econometrica*, 72(5):1329–76.

Martinez, S.-K., Meier, S. and Sprenger, C. (2022). Procrastination in the field: Evidence from tax filing. *Journal of the European Economics Association*, forthcoming.

Mas-Colell, A., Whinston, M. D. and Green, J. R. (1995). *Microeconomic Theory*. Oxford University Press.

McCaffery, E. J. and Slemrod, J. (2006). *Behavioral Public Finance*. Russell Sage Foundation.

Miller, B. M. and Mumford, K. J. (2015). The salience of complex tax changes: Evidence from the child and dependent care credit expansion. *National Tax Journal*, 68(3):477–510.

Mirrlees, J. (1971). An exploration in the theory of optimum income taxation. *The Review of Economic Studies*, 38(2):175–208.

Mirrlees, J. (1986). The theory of optimal taxation. *Handbook of Mathematical Economics*, volume 3, chapter 24, pages 1197–249. Elsevier.

Mortensen, D. (1986). Job search and labor market analysis. *Handbook of Labor Economics*, volume 2, chapter 15, pages 849–919. North-Holland.

Mueller, A. I., Spinnewijn, J. and Topa, G. (2021). Job seekers' perceptions and employment prospects: Heterogeneity, duration dependence, and bias. *American Economic Review*, 111(1):324–63.

Mullainathan, S., Schwartzstein, J. and Congdon, W. J. (2012). A reduced-form approach to behavioral public finance. *Annual Review of Economics*, 4(1):511–40.

Mullainathan, S. and Shafir, E. (2013). *Scarcity: Why Having Too Little Means So Much*. Allen Lane.

Nichols, A. N. and Zeckhauser, R. J. (1982). Targeting transfers through restrictions on recipients. *American Economic Review*, 72(2):372–7.

Nielsen, H. S., Sørensen, T. and Taber, C. (2010). Estimating the effect of student aid on college enrollment: Evidence from a government grant policy reform. *American Economic Journal: Economic Policy*, 2(2):185–215.

O'Donoghue, T. and Rabin, M. (1999). Doing it now or later. *American Economic Review*, 89(1):103–24.

OECD (2017). *Behavioural Insights and Public Policy.* https://read.oecd-ilibrary.org/governance/behavioural-insights-and-public-policy_9789264270480-en#page1.

Olafsson, A. and Pagel, M. (2017). The ostrich in us: Selective attention to financial accounts, income, spending, and liquidity. Working Paper 23945, National Bureau of Economic Research.

Piketty, T. (1997). La redistribution fiscale face au chômage. *Revue française d'économie*, 12(1).

Rabin, M. (2000). Risk aversion and expected-utility theory: A calibration theorem. *Econometrica*, 68(5):1281–92.

Rabin, M. (2002). A perspective on psychology and economics. *European Economic Review*, 46(4):657–85.

Rees-Jones, A. (2017). Quantifying loss-averse tax manipulation. *The Review of Economic Studies*, 85(2):1251–78.

Rees-Jones, A. and Taubinsky, D. (2018). Taxing humans: Pitfalls of the mechanism design approach and potential resolutions. *Tax Policy and the Economy*, 32(1):107–33.

Rees-Jones, A. and Taubinsky, D. (2020). Measuring 'schmeduling'. *The Review of Economic Studies*, 87(5):2399–438.

Rice, T. (2013). The behavioral economics of health and health care. *Annual Review of Public Health*, 34(1):431–47.

Rothschild, M. and Stiglitz, J. (1976). Equilibrium in competitive insurance markets: An essay on the economics of imperfect information. *The Quarterly Journal of Economics*, 90(4):629–49.

Saez, E. (2001). Using elasticities to derive optimal income tax rates. *Review of Economic Studies*, 68:205–29.

Saez, E. (2009). Details matter: The impact of presentation and information on the take-up of financial incentives for retirement saving. *American Economic Journal: Economic Policy*, 1(1):204–28.

Saez, E. (2010). Do taxpayers bunch at kink points? *American Economic Journal: Economic Policy*, 2(3):180–212.

Saez, E., Slemrod, J. and Giertz, S. H. (2012). The elasticity of taxable income with respect to marginal tax rates: A critical review. *Journal of Economic Literature*, 50(1):3–50.

Saez, E. and Stantcheva, S. (2016). Generalized social marginal welfare weights for optimal tax theory. *American Economic Review*, 106(1):24–45.

Salanié, B. (2011). *The Economics of Taxation*. MIT Press.

Sandroni, A. and Squintani, F. (2007). Overconfidence, insurance, and paternalism. *American Economic Review*, 97(5):1994–2004.

Schilbach, F. (2019). Alcohol and self-control: A field experiment in India. *American Economic Review*, 109(4):1290–322.

Schilbach, F., Schofield, H. and Mullainathan, S. (2016). The psychological lives of the poor. *American Economic Review*, 106(5):435–40.

Schmieder, J. F., von Wachter, T. and Bender, S. (2012a). The long-term effects of UI extensions on employment. *American Economic Review*, 102(3):514–19.

Schmieder, J. F., von Wachter, T. and Bender, S. (2012b). The effects of extended unemployment insurance over the business cycle: Evidence from regression discontinuity estimates over 20 years. *The Quarterly Journal of Economics*, 127(2):701–52.

Schmieder, J. F. and von Wachter, T. (2016). The effects of unemployment insurance benefits: New evidence and interpretation. *Annual Review of Economics*, 8:547–81.

Schmieder, J. F., von Wachter, T. and Bender, S. (2016). The effect of unemployment benefits and nonemployment durations on wages. *American Economic Review*, 106(3):739–77.

Schnellenbach, J. and Schubert, C. (2015). Behavioral political economy: A survey. *European Journal of Political Economy*, 40(PB):395–417.

Seibold, A. (2021). Reference points for retirement behavior: Evidence from German pension discontinuities. *American Economic Review*, 111(4): 1126–65.

Slemrod, J. (2007). Cheating ourselves: The economics of tax evasion. *Journal of Economic Perspectives*, 21(1):25–48.

Slemrod, J., Christian, C., London, R. and Parker, J. A. (1997). April 15 syndrome. *Economic Inquiry*, 35(4):695–709.

Slemrod, J. and Kopczuk, W. (2002). The optimal elasticity of taxable income. *Journal of Public Economics*, 84(1):91–112.

Spinnewijn, J. (2015). Unemployed but optimistic: Optimal insurance design with biased beliefs. *Journal of the European Economic Association*, 13(1):130–67.

Stantcheva, S. (2021). Understanding tax policy: How do people reason? *Quarterly Journal of Economics*, 136(4):2309–69.

Sunstein, C. R. (2014). *Why Nudge?: The Politics of Libertarian Paternalism*. Yale University Press.

Sunstein, C. R. and Thaler, R. H. (2009). *Nudge: Improving Decisions about Health, Wealth, and Happiness*. Penguin Books.

Taubinsky, D. and Rees-Jones, A. (2018). Attention variation and welfare: Theory and evidence from a tax salience experiment. *The Review of Economic Studies*, 85(4):2462–96.

Thaler, R. H. (1999). Mental accounting matters. *Journal of Behavioral Decision Making*, 12(3):183–206.

Thaler, R. H. and Sunstein, C. R. (2003). Libertarian paternalism. *American Economic Review*, 93(2):175–9.

Wooldridge, J. M. (2002). *Econometric Analysis of Cross Section and Panel Data*. MIT Press.

Behavioural and Experimental Economics

Nicolas Jacquemet

University Paris-1 Panthéon Sorbonne and the Paris School of Economics

Nicolas Jacquemet is a full professor at University Paris-1 Panthéon Sorbonne and the Paris School of Economics. His research combines experimental methods and econometrics to study discrimination, the effect of personality traits on economic behaviour, the role of social pre-involvement in strategic behaviour and experimental game theory. His research has been published in *Econometrica, Management Science, Games and Economic Behavior*, the *Journal of Environmental Economics and Management*, the *Journal of Health Economics*, and the *Journal of Economic Psychology*.

Olivier L'Haridon

Université de Rennes 1

Olivier L'Haridon is a full professor at the Université de Rennes I, France. His research combines experimental methods and decision theory, applied in the study of individual decision making as affected by uncertainty. His work has been published in *American Economic Review, Management Science*, the *Journal of Risk and Uncertainty, Theory and Decision, Experimental Economics*, the *Journal of Health Economics*, and the *Journal of Economic Psychology*.

About the Series

Cambridge Elements in Behavioural and Experimental Economics focuses on recent advances in two of the most important and innovative fields in modern economics. It aims to provide better understanding of economic behavior, choices, strategies and judgements, particularly through the design and use of laboratory experiments.

Cambridge Elements $^{\equiv}$

Behavioural and Experimental Economics

Printed in the United States
by Baker & Taylor Publisher Services